THE
CROSS

38,102 MILES
38 YEARS
ONE MISSION

THE
CROSS

ARTHUR BLESSITT

Authentic

COLORADO SPRINGS • MILTON KEYNES • HYDERABAD

Authentic Publishing
We welcome your questions and comments.

USA   1820 Jet Stream Drive, Colorado Springs, CO 80921 www.authenticbooks.com
UK   9 Holdom Avenue, Bletchley, Milton Keynes, Bucks, MK1 1QR
         www.authenticmedia.co.uk
India   Logos Bhavan, Medchal Road, Jeedimetla Village, Secunderabad 500 055, A.P.

The Cross
ISBN-13: 978-1-934068-67-0

10 09 08 / 6 5 4 3 2 1

Published in 2008 by Authentic

A catalog record for this book is available through the Library of Congress.

Editorial team: Steve Rabey, Andy Sloan, Dana Bromley, Dan Johnson

Printed in the United States of America

CONTENTS

Dedication

I would like to dedicate this book to my parents, Arthur and Mary Virginia Blessitt. They are both in heaven now, but when I was a child they helped me come to Jesus and learn how to follow him. They always encouraged me to do the will of God. I honor them.

I dedicate this book also to my wife, Denise Irja Blessitt—the most profound and godly woman I have ever known. She has traveled the world with me and with the cross in almost 290 nations and island groups. Her total commitment to Jesus, her courageous spirit, and her incredible love for me and the people of this world have inspired me and strengthened me. She is fearless yet tender, full of joy and passion. Without her I do not believe I could have completed the call to carry the cross in every nation. I am thrilled to be in her presence and to have the awesome joy of living my life with her.

I am delighted to dedicate this book to my seven children as well: Gina, Joel, Joy, Joshua, Joseph, Jerusalem, and Sophia. I am blessed to have lived with them on the roadsides of the world. They never complained of what they were missing but loved all the people of the world we met; and they love their dad. They have blessed me with eight adorable grandchildren.

I want to dedicate this book to the Arthur Blessitt Evangelistic Association board directors, both present and past, who have loved and faithfully supported the mission and call of Jesus on my life: Pastors Gwin and Norma Turner, Fred Roach, Ken Wolfe, Pete Cantrell, Claude Townsend, and Owen Cooper. They have been wise and godly counselors.

I dedicate this book to all the beautiful people of the world who welcomed us into their homes. To all the armies of the world I met in times of war, yet they let the cross pass in peace. To the many thousands of people who gave me something to eat or drink. To those who cared for my children and my wife in distant lands. I close my eyes, and as the tears flood I see the faces of countless people I have met and whose hands I have held and whose heads I have touched to bless. I love you all; I miss you; I trust to see you all in heaven. You cared for a pilgrim stranger passing your way—and in so doing you will receive the same reward as I.

A group of people, numbering only in the hundreds, supported us financially on this cross-walk around the world. They are the ones who have given and prayed and helped us on our journeys with their money. The cost over the past thirty-eight years has been staggering, but from their gifts they paid for our plane tickets, lodging, transport, supplies, and medical expenses. They prayed for us and loved us and encouraged us. I dedicate this book to them. Thank you.

One man has been a key adviser and has stayed in touch with Denise and me for so many years as we travel the world. He calls and checks on us and is ready to do whatever is needed. Thanks, Buddy Gaster. I also dedicate this book to you.

I also want to dedicate this book to Steve Johnson, global publisher, IBS-STL/Authentic Media; and Volney James, publisher, Authentic Books, who approached me about doing this book. Only through their help and persistence was this book possible. Thanks, also, to Steve and Lois Rabey for their help in writing the book and to Andrew Sloan, who did an awesome job of editing the book and getting it ready for publication.

I am fortunate to have had the best support team in the world. I have lived the most blessed life. Thank you all. God bless you. Enjoy the book. You helped make it possible. I love you.

Thanks most of all to God the Father, to Jesus the Son, and to the Holy Spirit—who have been with me every step around the world and to whom all honor and glory are due!

Chapter 1

One Step at a Time

FIRST DAY,

Hollywood, America

The sounds of the city night fill my ears, and the memories of today fill my mind. My aching, pained body and my blistered feet remind me of my humanity.

I never dreamed carrying a cross would be like this, Lord.

Oh, I need you, Jesus. Have mercy on me. I've never been a sportsman, and now I'm heading across America. I'm thrilled! I feel the excitement of the unknown, and I'm ready to take the Jesus Movement from coast to coast. It's also frightening, but I will not be deterred from your will.

You are with me and your presence is enough. It's been a wild day but people prayed and I can still smile.

I love you, Lord.

LAST DAY,

Zanzibar, Africa

My emotions almost overcome me as I lie tonight by the sea. The walk is complete and I am alive.

I will miss, oh, I will miss, the long walks with just you and me along the roadsides of the world, Lord. You, Jesus, have been my constant companion, and I can hardly conceive of living without our intimate times on the road or at night on the roadsides. There is nothing like being with you with the wind in my face in a distant land or feeling your presence in the midst of danger and conflict.

CERTIFICATE

The greatest distance claimed for a "round the world" pilgrimage is 60,353 km (37,502 miles) by Arthur Blessitt (USA) since 25 December 1969. He has visited all seven continents, including Antarctica, having crossed 310 nations, island groups and territories carrying a 3.7-m-tall (12-ft) wooden cross and preaching from the Bible throughout his pilgrimage.

GUINNESS WORLD RECORDS LTD

It's been a long journey around the world, but my heart feels young and my body fresh. You know, Jesus, I feel better than I did that first day thirty-eight years ago.

Today at early dawn you asked me to lie on the cross. I did not want to do this, I never had before, but I obeyed you. You reminded me of the Scripture "I am crucified with Christ: nevertheless I live; not I, but Christ lives in me" (Galatians 2:20, my paraphrase). As tears washed my face, I cried so hard I could hardly breathe. You said, "The world is open to you; you are free to carry the cross and minister Jesus in all the world, wherever I lead you."

As of the publication of this book, I have carried a cross more than thirty-eight thousand miles through 315 nations and island groups in all seven continents of the world. That number includes every sovereign nation and every major island group in the world. The *Guinness Book of Records* has recorded my walking milestones since 1996, when it recognized me for making "the world's longest walk." The *Guinness World Records 2000: Millennium Edition* dedicated a page to this achievement, including a picture of me carrying my cross.

Over the past four decades I have visited sacred sites and bloody battlefields. I have been applauded as well as pelted by stones. I have shared Christ alongside Billy Graham and twice preached to crowds of half-a-million people. I have been arrested or thrown into jail two dozen times.

I have slept in the presidential suites of fancy hotels as well as a pigpen in Colombia. I have survived numerous auto crashes. Snakes, baboons, elephants, and crocodiles have attacked me. And I have been hauled before a firing squad to be shot and killed.

Recently someone asked me, "How do you walk around the entire world?"

"One step at a time," I replied.

Throughout my life, I have heard hundreds of people talk about the dreams they wanted to pursue, the projects they wanted to complete, and the things God called them to do. But many times these projects don't go forward. Why?

Because people don't take one step at a time. They don't break big things down into small, simple steps. As a result they are soon overcome with the insurmountable challenges that face them, and they give up.

Experience has taught me that when God gives us a vision for what we should do with our lives we need to break that vision down into simple steps. That's what happened to me. And I believe that if you will dream big but start small, your dreams will come to fruition. Let me explain what I mean.

Reaching an Unreached Generation

In the 1960s God called me to minister to hippies, Hell's Angels, runaways, drug addicts, teen prostitutes, flower children, would-be actors and rock stars, and other young people who were part of the emerging youth scene in Hollywood, California. Answering this call was an important step for me to take.

In 1966 and 1967 young people staged "love-ins" each Sunday at Griffith Park. I would talk to them about Jesus as they sat in the grass, listening to bands, taking LSD, and drinking.

One Sunday a young man asked me, "Why don't you present your message from on stage?"

"They probably wouldn't let me," I said, looking toward the platform where a psychedelic rock group played loud, screeching music.

"Sure you can," he said. "I run the program. You can have five minutes."

I spoke briefly about Jesus from the platform and was greeted with warm applause. I invited those who wanted to hear more to meet me under a nearby tree. About fifty came over to talk with me.

This was my first big step in becoming known as "the minister of Sunset Strip." And as I would see throughout my life, when I reached out to people in love with the message of Jesus, many would listen and respond.

I walked the streets of Hollywood, talking to kids, feeding them, and allowing twenty or more to sleep on the floor of my apartment at night. I also preached at some of the nightclubs on Sunset Strip, including Gazzarri's, one of the strip's most famous clubs. I would preach at Gazzarri's, and musicians such as Andrae Crouch and The Disciples, Charles McPheeters and The New Creatures, Sharon Peck and The Sunshine Sisters, and the Jimmy Owens Singers would perform.

I was ministering to the lonely, the embittered, the lost, and the hopeful who flocked by the thousands to Sunset Strip each week. But I felt we needed a place of our own. My prayers were answered in March 1968 when His Place opened in the heart of Sunset Strip in a rented building next door to a topless go-go club.

His Place had wild stage lights, fishnet material on the ceiling, a quiet prayer room, and a pool table. But something was missing: there was no cross. I felt we needed a life-sized cross hanging on the wall near the stage so that everyone who walked in would be immediately affected. Young people stoned on drugs or drunk might forget everything I told them, but I felt certain they would never forget the cross.

An electric company in Santa Monica gave us big wooden cable spools, which we used as tables. We also got some large wooden beams that were used for light poles. These beams were soaked in creosote to preserve them. I felt they would also make the perfect "old rugged cross" for His Place.

But even before we finished putting the cross together from the rough wood, we witnessed the impact it would have on the young people on the strip.

From Hell's Angel to Heaven's Child

After drilling a hole and inserting a bolt, we realized that we didn't have a wrench to tighten the bolt. Just at that moment I heard the roar of a Harley-Davidson. Looking out the front window of His Place, I saw Tom, a local biker, getting off his chopper. I knew Tom from my times of sharing Christ with the Hell's Angels. He was as tough as they come, with strong shoulders, a bushy beard, and long hair.

"Hey, Tom!" I called. "Do you have a wrench I can borrow? It will only take a minute."

"Yeah," he said. "I got one."

I reached to take the wrench, but Tom had another idea. "I'll do it for you," he said, following me into His Place. But he froze in his steps once he saw the cross, which was twelve feet tall and six feet long, lying on the floor.

"What's that?" he asked.

"It's a cross."

"Hey, man, you do it," he said, backing away from the cross.

"Okay," I replied. "But will you come back tonight and see it on the wall?"

"No, I'm not coming back," he said, shaking his head and staring at the cross.

"Well, come back sometime," I said. "Jesus loves you, Tom. This cross is not the message of death, but life. Jesus died for you and rose again. You can have real life in him. You can be free inside."

"No," Tom sighed, "I don't want nothing to do with the cross."

"Hey, man, you are already a part of it," I said. "Your wrench tightened down the center bolt!"

But Tom turned and walked away. After he left, we knelt around the cross, dedicating it to Jesus and praying for Tom.

Four days later Tom walked into His Place and stared at the cross hanging on the wall.

"Tom, Jesus loves you," I said softly.

"You know," Tom said, "I just can't get this cross out of my mind. Everywhere I go I keep seeing it lying there on the floor. I even dreamed about it. It's strange how I drove up just at the time you needed that wrench."

I replied, "No, it's not strange at all—because Jesus wants you. He is drawing you to himself. Open your heart, and you can know him. Repent, and he will cleanse you."

Tom nodded, and the two of us went to the prayer room, where I showed him passages from the Bible about Jesus' saving love. As we prayed together, Tom was born into the family of God.

During the next two weeks I spent much time talking, studying, and praying with Tom. Then tragedy hit. Tom's motorcycle was struck on the Hollywood Freeway, and he was killed. When I preached at his funeral, five more bikers came to know Jesus.

Others would have similar encounters with the cross at His Place, but I will always remember the impact it had on Tom.

The Cross on the Move

Around five o'clock one morning I knelt by my bed and prayed. I was twenty-eight years old and would soon be twenty-nine. Suddenly Jesus spoke to me, not in an audible voice, but in my heart and mind. He said: *I want you to take the cross that is hanging on the wall in His*

Place and carry it across America.

I was stunned. But then the joy of the Lord washed over me like ocean waves. Tears poured down my face, yet I was smiling and thanking Jesus for reaching out to me.

Then the Lord spoke more: *I want you to take the cross into the roadsides and streets to identify my message in the streets with the common man. I am sending you into the secular world. I am going to put the gospel on television, on the radio, by your walking. I want you to bear witness to my life and my love, proclaim my peace in the streets.*

As I reflected on these things, it seemed the Lord was telling me: *When I was here, I was in the streets with the common man. And that is where my message has to be identified again—in the streets.*

All this surprised me, but I didn't question it. Instead, I was thrilled that Christ had spoken to *me*! Many times throughout history, God has called the good, the mighty, and the best-qualified people to serve him. This time God reached down to the bottom of the barrel and found me.

Blessitt—come on, boy, I could hear him saying.

Okay, Lord, I said, happy and thrilled to be doing anything he wanted me to do.

A Potential Setback

I could hardly wait to get going on my cross-country walk with the cross. But before I could take my first step, I received some bad news about my health.

Lying in a hospital bed in Glendale Adventist Medical Center, I heard the doctor's grim prognosis: "Mr. Blessitt, you need brain surgery immediately. You have an aneurysm in your brain—an abnormal dilation of the blood vessel wall, a blood vessel blown out like a balloon. This is seeping blood, causing your problem."

Four times in three years I had experienced problems with my health. Sometimes I became numb on much of the right side of my body. This time a stroke had landed me in the hospital, leading to a battery of tests.

"We need to operate immediately and repair these blood vessels," continued the doctor. "This is a very serious operation, and you should be okay in a couple of months. But I should also warn you there is a possibility you could die or be paralyzed during the operation."

"What if I don't have the surgery?" I asked.

"The blood vessels could burst at any time. If you just rest, don't get excited, don't preach, and don't lift heavy things, you may have from six months to three years to live. But the aneurysm must be repaired."

There I was. On the one hand, the doctor said to "operate." On the other hand, God had told me to "carry the cross." Should I obey the doctor or the call of God? I asked the doctor for some time to consider my options, and I returned home.

I prayed and prayed before coming to a conclusion that would shape the rest of my life. What had changed since Jesus called me to carry the cross? Only my circumstances were different. Right then I concluded that I should not let circumstances alter the call of Jesus. The call of God is not conditional. I decided that I would rather die in the will of God than live outside of it. If I carried the cross, I would be at peace whether I lived or died. But if I stayed home, I knew I would rot inside from a mixture of doubt, fear, and the knowledge that I had refused the call of God.

Faith and reason had wrestled in my heart. Faith won, and I would never look back. I have had to contend with numbness in my body on and off over the years, but it hasn't kept me from fulfilling Jesus' call to walk with the cross.

I had decided to go, but I wasn't foolish enough to think I would not meet further opposition.

One Final Hurdle

On Christmas morning in 1969, about two hundred people gathered around His Place to bid farewell to me and to the team accompanying me on our journey from Los Angeles to Washington, D.C.

For several years my call had been to minister in Hollywood by sharing Jesus with the people and by helping them experience salvation and become followers of Jesus. A great revolution had started there. Now Jesus was calling me to take another step: to go across America. I didn't know it at the time, but this new ministry would help spread the Jesus Movement across the country.

My pastor, Gwin Turner, was there in a suit and tie. Around him stood kids who were stoned on drugs; braless, runaway girls; motorcycle and street gang leaders; young men from the criminal underworld; several other followers of Jesus; and the His Place staff.

Pastor Turner laid hands on me to anoint me for the pilgrimage ahead. I took the cross from inside the building, raised it to my right shoulder, and yelled to the crowd, "Give me a J!"

"J," they shouted back.

"Give me an E!"

"E," they yelled.

They continued repeating the letters after me until I shouted, "What does that spell?"

"JESUS!"

"Who does America need?"

"JESUS!"

Then, as I walked with the cross along Sunset Boulevard, a man rushed up to us and started screaming. "That's my cross!" he hollered as he grabbed at the cross and tried to pull it off my shoulder. "I want it back! It's mine!"

I knew Jesus told his disciples that if anyone asked them for their shirt, they should give their coat also. But what's a person to do when a yelling man is trying to take your cross?

Finally the man stopped his struggle and issued a threat. "I'll be back soon," he said. "And when I get back here, I will kill you all."

Half an hour later the man reappeared. This time he was carrying a big board with a long nail driven through it, and he was waving the board and screaming, "I'm going to kill you!"

There we were. Jim McPheeters was a physically fit marine who had just returned from Vietnam and had been converted to Jesus at His Place. O. J. Peterson was a former alcoholic and nightclub piano player. And Jessie Wise was a muscular, former black militant. This team would walk across America with me. And because I was pretty strong myself,

I felt that together the four of us could take on this madman.

But Jesus had another idea. I heard the Lord speaking to my heart: *If you are going to carry the cross, are you willing to live in the way of the cross?* As the man rushed toward us, these words rang in my ears.

"Fellows, we can't touch him," I said. "We've never used violence before, and we can't start now. If we live, we live. If we die, we die. If you can't take it, run as fast as you can. But we can't lay a finger on this man."

As the man started to hit me with the board, I cried out, "In Jesus' name, in Jesus' name." But I didn't move.

Jim stepped between the man and me, ready to accept the blows. Looking at the man, he said, "In Jesus' name, I love you."

The next thing we knew the man seemed unable to move his hands. He stood there shaking, his face a mixture of hate and fear.

"Fellows, let's pray," I said. We wrapped our arms around the cross and knelt there on the sidewalk.

"In the name of Jesus, let this man know you love him, just as we love him," we said.

"Lord, if we live, we live for you. If we die, we die for you."

As we prayed and resigned ourselves to the will of God, I once again felt waves of joy washing over me, just as I felt when Jesus first called me to carry the cross. The next thing I knew, I heard the sound of weeping. The man was on his knees, the board lying at his side.

"Sir," I said, "God loves you. Jesus died for you. Ask him into your heart."

"Get out of here!" he screamed. "Leave me alone!"

I tried to talk more, but he continued to scream. "Go on," he yelled. "God is with you! Take the cross and go."

We picked up the cross and started walking. We didn't know what else we would encounter as we walked from Los Angeles to Washington D.C., but we knew we wouldn't be bored! We ended up walking about thirty-five hundred miles between Hollywood and Washington, D.C., weaving our way there as we walked through many major cities and often used secondary roads rather than freeways.

Not long after we walked across America, Jesus led me to carry the cross from nation to nation. Then, in 1988, Jesus called me to give my life to carry the cross in every nation before the year 2000.

Make It Simple

Has God called you to do something for him? If so, don't think about what everything will be like when your mission is accomplished. Start by thinking of where your first step will take you.

What did Jesus do when he came to reach humanity? He started small and simple. He called twelve unsophisticated fishermen to be his disciples and commissioned them to preach the gospel to the ends of the world.

Over the years I have made many TV appearances on the Trinity Broadcasting Network (TBN). Paul Crouch, who founded TBN, built radios in his bedroom when he was a kid. When he attended college, he created an amateur radio station in his dorm room. Today TBN reaches around the world. But if Paul had thought about that at the beginning, he probably would have been paralyzed by doubt and fear. Instead he took small steps, one after another.

You may never walk around the world carrying a cross. But I know God does have something he would like you to do. And the only way you are going to fulfill this calling is by starting out simple and following his call, step by step by step.

Chapter 2

Where Should I Go? What Should I Do?

SAUDI ARABIA

The sand was hot, but my face was cooled with tears of joy as today Denise and I lifted up

your cross, Jesus, in this land. They said it couldn't be done, but you led us like you led me as a child; turn left, turn right, and we made it in

The cross was lifted up, and we claimed your land. This desert shall bloom in the glory of the Lord.

I can hardly believe my darling wife volunteered to stay behind to guarantee my return Oh, how fearless she is! Her commitment continues to amaze me.

Those guards were so kind, their hospitality

so touching and their hearts so open to love. And, yes, I dream of Saudi filled with churches, children singing in the streets, and women free to drive and live and love. I dream of freedom filling every heart with the good news of Jesus going forth and finding its home in every person. No walls. No barriers. Nothing can stop your will, oh Lord.

You, Lord, are the Lord of Hosts, and mighty is your name, and glorious are your ways. It sure was an adventure over those sand dunes under the scorching sun, and we made it! What a powerful day of victory. It's all about you, Jesus. I can only smile and lift my hands in praise for the glory of this day.

S on, I don't care what you think Jesus told you to do. I want you to do what I told you to do!"

I could see anger written on my father's face. The conflict was a simple one. Dad had given me a job to do. But even though I was not quite eight years old, I was claiming that God had given me a different assignment.

As I think back on it now, I can see that this episode many years ago was a crucial fork in the road for me. I went down the road I believed God wanted me to travel, and that decision has made all the difference in my life.

Water of Life

When I was a boy, my father managed a large cotton farm in northeast Louisiana, out in the country near a town called Oak Grove and just down the road from the tiny community of Goodwill.

The farm covered acres and acres of rich, fertile soil that had been recovered from swampland. During the summer growing season, dozens of migrant workers from Mexico chopped down the grass and weeds that had grown among the cotton plants. Then later, during the fall, as many as one hundred workers walked up and down the rows, picking the fluffy white cotton from the plants and stuffing it into big cloth bags.

It was hard work, made even harder by the burning sun and high humidity. Often my dad told me to deliver water to the workers so they could ease their thirst and replace the sweat that seemed to pour out of their bodies as they chopped away at grass and weeds.

I remember one morning during the late summer of 1948 when Jesus began answering my prayers for guidance in a most unusual way. I was dressed in Big Mac overalls and a plaid shirt, and I was wearing a big straw hat to keep the blistering sun off my body. I carried two metal buckets filled with water, one with my right hand and the other with my left. As I walked barefoot through the fields, I could hear the water sloshing around in the buckets, but metal lids kept it from spilling out onto the ground.

Usually my father directed me toward a group of workers whom

I could see chopping away as I looked over the tops of the cotton plants. The water buckets were heavy, so the sensible thing would have been to walk straight across the field to the workers. Even at the age of seven, I knew that the shortest distance between two points is a straight line.

But apparently God had another idea. As I walked across the field in the heat and humidity with my buckets of water, I felt Jesus speaking to me. It is difficult to explain exactly how I knew, but I felt within my spirit and my mind that Jesus was telling me to follow him.

The path he chose was not a straight line that made the most sense to me. Instead, I was to walk forward thirteen steps, then turn right and go another twenty steps, and then turn to the left four more steps. As I obeyed each prompting, he continued to lead me around the field. Day after day as I carried the water, I sensed Jesus telling me where to go and where to turn.

These directions made no sense to me. And there were times when all I wanted to do was get to the workers, deliver the water, and sit down in the shade to rest from my wandering. But for some reason I never doubted that Jesus was speaking to me—even when I wound up at a tree far from the choppers or when I seemed to go around in circles for half an hour. Even when Jesus' commands made no sense to me, I could not shake the conviction that I was in God's hands, going where he directed me.

One day as I was walking in a field, I saw Dad's truck in the distance. He spotted me and drove into one of the many paths that cut across the fields. From the look on his face, I could tell I was in trouble.

Years later my father dedicated his life fully to Christ, but at that time he struggled with a drinking problem, which added elements of anger and violence to our lives. When he got close enough for me to hear him, he said some words I won't repeat in this book. But the point of his message was this: "What the heck are you doing, Son? The thirsty men are way over there at the other side of the field, but you are over here wandering around."

"Well," I said, "Jesus told me to come over here. He told me to turn right and turn left, so that's what I did."

A look of anger came over my father's face as he yelled at me, pointed me in a straight line toward the workers, and demanded that I deliver the water to them in record time. "And if I ever catch you doing this again, I will give you a spanking you will never forget!"

At that point I started crying and stammering. I didn't understand why my dad was so mad. After all, I was only doing what Jesus told me to do. As I started toward the men, I looked over my shoulder and said to Dad, "Jesus told me to do this. I don't want to be over here anyway." Then I cried out to God: "What should I do now? You led me over there, and I got in trouble for it!"

And as I walked across the field, hearing the sounds of sloshing water, I sensed Jesus speaking to my heart: *You should obey your dad. But realize that I'm training you to hear my voice and obey me so you will be able to go where I'm leading you.*

Throughout the rest of the summer, I went straight to the workers whenever my father was nearby. But when he was in town or in the barn working on a tractor, I would listen for God's prompting and go where he told me to go.

Little did I realize the experiences I had in the cotton fields that summer would prepare me for a life of following God around the world. I emerged from that summer having learned a lesson that would stay with me for the rest of my life. Right then I decided I would rather obey God and become a fool in other people's eyes than fail to do what he was telling me to do. And I have never regretted that decision.

Two Big Questions

All of us need to figure out how we will spend our lives. What goals will we pursue? To which things will we give a greater priority? Which tasks will we attack with the most urgency? And which ideas will we simply ignore or neglect?

Since that Louisiana summer many, many years ago, I have been consumed with asking Jesus what *he* wants me to do with my life. I have repeatedly asked him these two questions:

Where do you want me to go?

What do you want me to do?

Duty in the Desert

Fast-forward to 1998—fifty years after my experiences in the cotton fields—and I am sitting at a desk with a stack of world maps. Once again I am asking Jesus these two questions:

Where do you want me to go?

What do you want me to do?

Over the years I had visited all of the sovereign nations in the world except two: Saudi Arabia and North Korea. Denise and I had been applying for visas to both countries for years. These applications had gone unanswered, but I felt I was being directed to take the cross to these countries.

In 1998 very few Americans visited Saudi Arabia. The Saudis are devout Muslims, and it was within the borders of their nation that the prophet Muhammad was born. Activity by Christian churches is forbidden and Bibles are banned, making this one of the most challenging nations in the world to walk with a cross. Most foreign tourists are not allowed entrance there. Only businesspeople, laborers with visas, and Muslim pilgrims participating in the annual haj (or pilgrimage) are granted entry.

As Denise and I discussed our inability to get a visa for Saudi Arabia, she looked at me with her tender yet strong eyes and said, "Let's go anyway; Jesus will show us the way."

Then, as I prayed, Jesus spoke to me very clearly: *Go to Dubai, then to Abu Dhabi, and then on toward Saudi Arabia. Turn left; then go right. That is the way in.*

Traveling to Saudi Arabia with a cross is more complicated than carrying buckets of water to workers in cotton fields, but the principle is the same. If God calls you and sends you, he will show you the way. After we had studied maps and every possible route to Saudi Arabia, Jesus showed us the way to get in.

We rented a car in Dubai, tied the cross onto the top of it, and began driving through the United Arab Emirates (UAE), a coalition of seven oil-rich states. After hours of driving in 102-degree temperatures through the desert and through Abu Dhabi, we arrived at the Liwa Oasis in the heart of the desert. As we followed God's leading concerning when we should turn left and then right, we found ourselves at the end of the paved road. Surrounded by huge sand dunes, we were now driving on a sand road. This was certainly four-wheel-drive country—a road for trucks heading for the oil fields—but we were in a car! We prayed, and I increased our speed so we could keep moving in the soft sand. We would slip and slide as if we were on ice, but the Lord helped us keep going.

After hours of navigating the shifting sands, we arrived at a building that looked like a fort. It was the local police station and a border checkpoint for the UAE. We wanted to find out how far we were from the Saudi border, so we approached the office and inquired. A police officer had another man take us to an air-conditioned room where men were sitting on the floor, drinking tea, and eating. The men invited us to share their food, tea, and cigarettes, showing that hospitality is truly a universal language.

I showed the men some photos I carry with me from my previous trips. They were particularly interested in the photos of me standing next to Palestinian Liberation Organization leader Yasser Arafat or Libyan leader Muammar al-Gadhafi. The men in the room knew I was a follower of Jesus, but they were impressed that I had met and talked with these leaders who are respected among Muslims.

As we sat and chatted with the men, we explained our mission of carrying the cross in Saudi Arabia. We were shocked when one of the men told us, "Saudi Arabia is just there! When you leave this station you are in Saudi!"

When Denise realized we were so close, she made a courageous offer to the men. She told them she would stay in the station to guarantee my return if they would let me cross the border and carry the cross into Saudi Arabia. After talking to each other in Arabic for a moment, they came back with an even better offer. They would let us both cross the border, but they would keep our passports as an assurance that we would return as we promised. They even seemed excited to help us do so.

We thanked Jesus for making the way for us and got in our car, which quickly became stuck in a huge sand dune a few yards from the border. But the men from the station got a truck and pulled us out so we could continue our journey. After we drove a short distance, the shifting sand gave way to a paved road that seemed out of place in this remote desert wilderness. We followed the road until we came to a place where we could park and I could bolt the cross together.

The hot wind blew sand in my eyes as I carried the cross. Denise drove alongside and filmed me as I walked.

I climbed a high sand dune and stood the cross straight up. For me this was a powerful symbol, seeing the cross lifted up in this land. Lying in the sand, I prayed for God to bless Saudi Arabia and grant its people liberty to hear the gospel. Then I opened my Bible and read a passage from the prophet Isaiah: "A voice of one calling: 'In the desert prepare the way for the LORD; make straight in the wilderness a highway for our God. Every valley shall be raised up, every mountain and hill made low; the rough ground shall become level, the rugged places a plain. And the glory of the LORD will be revealed, and all mankind together will see it. For the mouth of the LORD has spoken'" (Isaiah 40:3–5).

As I prayed at the foot of the cross, I felt God telling me that our mission in Saudi Arabia was completed. After years of waiting and after driving twelve hours across 560 miles of desert sand in the baking heat, we had finally carried the cross in this nation.

Once again, Jesus told me where he wanted me to go. He told me what he wanted me to do. And he opened the way for this to happen.

We returned to the border post, picked up our passports, thanked the guards for their help, and prayed for them.

For Those Who Have Ears to Hear

A frightening thing happened in 1983 when I was carrying the cross in Greece with my son Joshua and our team. At the end of a very long day of walking we asked an old man if we could sleep behind his house in our sleeping bags. He said yes and showed us a smooth place in his yard where we could stay. We all went quickly to sleep.

The next thing I knew, our restful night was interrupted by a frightening sound. I had the feeling the whole world was falling apart. The noise and shaking and rumbling were so strong that I thought we were in the middle of an earthquake. We leaped up in panic, as the sound and shaking grew stronger. But then we heard a train whistle and the telltale sound of steel wheels on iron tracks. This was no earthquake—we had been sleeping next to a railroad track!

The next morning we asked our Greek host how he could sleep through such noise. He laughed and responded, but the only word we could understand was "normal." The sound and fury of the nightly train were as normal to him as the sound of crickets is to me.

Unfortunately, I think some people have become so accustomed to not hearing the voice of God that this absence of guidance is a normal state for them. God may be trying to get their attention and guide them, as he was when I carried water in the cotton fields, but they have closed their ears and hardened their hearts. After years of tuning God out, they wonder why they can't hear God speak to them when they pray or when they ask for guidance at a crucial moment in their lives.

The apostle Paul wrote, "Let us also walk in the Spirit" (Galatians 5:25 NKJV). The Greek word *stoicheo* means "to walk in line," much like a marching soldier or a member of a marching band would do. This is a good picture of how we should follow God's leading today. Walking in the Spirit means to be in step with the Spirit. We are to walk in step with the Holy Spirit's guidance. And this begins with listening; so when the Spirit says to go left, we are to immediately turn left.

This is how I have sought to live my life, and it's the way you can live your life too. God may not be sending you to Saudi Arabia; but he has things he wants you to do. Are you listening for his call?

A lesson I have learned over the years is a simple one. The most important decision you will ever make will be the response you make to the next thing God calls you to do. It's not about what you did or didn't do twenty years ago. It's not about what you think you might or might not do ten years from now. It's about asking God the two questions we noted at the beginning of this chapter and obeying the promptings the Lord gives you:

> Where do you want me to go?
> What do you want me to do?

Try asking these questions every moment of every day and listening for the answer you receive. You will be amazed at where you will go and what you will do.

Chapter 3

The Shadow of the Cross

Then Jesus said to his disciples, "If anyone would come after me, he must deny himself and take up his cross and follow me."
—Matthew 16:24

POLAND AND THE PEOPLE
<u>FLOCKING TO THE CROSS</u>

I can see only streams of people. I can feel only love. I can live only in this moment of unexplainable glory. I can hear only the voices of thousands welcoming Jesus; I never want to live any other way.

If time could only stand still and this day would last forever.

Oh Lord, how beautiful these people are. They are so hungry for you and your ways. I can think only that it was something like this

when you, Jesus, were walking in the fields, streets, and towns. The people flooded to you, touched and reached out to you. And they found life in you.

Help me Jesus to never forget the passion of

these people. May I learn from them and carry their love in my heart always. They have risen above the oppression; they have loved the cross. They shall see a new day. I know it. I can feel it. Help me to see your beauty, Lord, and not the ugly face of evil.

I can hardly contain the exploding joy of my spirit within my body. The road behind me helps me to better travel the road ahead. I am lying in this barn on the hay and look forward to the new day about to dawn. I can see the smiling faces and the weeping eyes rushing to the cross!

The cross is perhaps the most well-known symbol in the world. From its origin as an instrument of suffering and death it has become—through the suffering and death of Jesus Christ—a symbol of life, love, hope, and salvation. On the third day Jesus arose and ascended to the Father, and now he ever lives to make intercession for us. The good news of the gospel is focused on the cross and the shed blood of Jesus for our sins.

I have had the humbling privilege of giving well over half my life to the calling of carrying the cross from nation to nation. I've walked tens of millions of steps. This has been a journey not just of walking, but of walking with a cross—feeling its weight and hearing people's love or reproach for the cross.

Today, as I was thinking about this chapter, I took a walk with the cross. The sun was shining brightly, so I could see the shadow of me carrying the cross as I moved along the street. Tears filled my eyes as I remembered tough days in the jungles or deserts or war zones. I remembered walking in rain, in snow, in heat, and in cold. I remembered people coming to the cross and finding new life and salvation. And, yes, there have been rejections, but I choose not to magnify those occasions. In the shadow of the cross I have lived, traveled the world, raised seven children, and found welcome and love all around the world.

I am encouraged by what Jesus is doing today. After having carried the cross in every nation, I can say that the world is open to and hungry for the good news of Jesus and the cross. The only problem is that the laborers are few, as Jesus said.

As I complete this mission, I feel peace. Jesus is ruling and reigning in the world today. The church is triumphant, and people around the globe are welcoming Jesus. In the shadow of the cross you see firsthand the glorious kingdom of God all around the world. You see the suffering and resurrection of Jesus that have the power to set us free and change our lives. As followers of Jesus, we face great challenges. But Jesus is with us, and he has all power.

I have also felt the agony of the cross as I walked among people suffering from war, hunger, injustice, and oppression. Tears often wash my face as I walk. The weight of the burden of the lost and suffering is heavier than the physical weight of the cross. Yet I walk on . . .

Pain and Passion

Mel Gibson's film *The Passion of the Christ* gave many people a new understanding of Jesus' journey to the cross and the horror of his crucifixion. As I've walked, I've often wondered what thoughts were in Christ's mind as he walked toward his crucifixion. Jesus died as a sacrifice for our sins on the cross he carried. I carry the cross to remind people of that incomprehensible sacrifice.

I also wonder what thoughts were in the mind of Simon from Cyrene, who Scripture tells us also carried the cross of Jesus, as he shouldered the wooden cross and made his way beside Jesus through the narrow streets and out the gate to the Place of the Skull. How did Simon feel as he walked beside the bleeding Christ?

While I don't know for sure what Jesus or Simon thought, I do know that carrying the cross has shaped not only my life but also my physical body. The weight of the cross restricts the blood supply to my arm, so I have to give my right shoulder (my preferred side) a break by moving the cross to my left shoulder from time to time. After years of bearing the weight of the cross, my right shoulder bone has developed about one inch of growth.

Perhaps I'm the only person in history who has been physically shaped by the weight of a cross. But the changes the cross has brought to my physical body are not important. What is important is how the cross has changed my life, and the lives of so many others, from the inside out. I pray that the spiritual weight of the cross has shaped my life according to the example of Jesus.

Poland: A People of the Cross

As I journey around the world, I find the cross to be a universal symbol of God's love that can be understood in spite of language and cultural barriers.

One of the most wonderful responses came from Poland, where I carried the cross each year from 1981 to 1984. The welcome I received in Poland and the understanding the people had for me and this pilgrimage with the cross are the greatest I have ever known. When I looked into their eyes, we connected instantly. They could see the struggle, the hurt, and the living faith in me, and I could feel their struggle and hurt and see their battle for faith.

The Polish people understood the cross as no other nation I have been through. They were not ashamed of the cross; they were true friends of the cross. They have enriched my life and taught me so much.

At Heathrow Airport in London, England, I checked in my cross, and they put a baggage claim ticket around it, not asking a word. It was as if everyone checked in twelve-foot crosses!

As I boarded the plane, I realized no one would meet me at the airport in Warsaw. Nobody knew I was coming. Yet, as I settled into my seat, knowing it was going to be just the Lord and me, I felt the glory of his presence. I felt an excitement and expectancy greater than any other in life. I love to live on the edge.

Many people say, "If I didn't have security, I'd die. I want security." But I don't want security—other than the security of knowing that I love and am loved by both my Lord and my family.

I arrived in Warsaw and made it through the immigration checkpoint. This was my first visit to a communist country, so when a person from the customs office approached me, I wasn't sure what to expect. She looked at my cross and asked, "What is this?"

"It's a cross," I answered.

"Are you going to take it with you when you leave Poland, or are you going to leave it in Poland?"

"I'll be taking it with me."

She then wrote on the back of my travel paper, in Polish: "Brought in one cross, can take out one cross."

The Power of the Cross

What happened next has happened in many countries: people flocked to the cross. They ran and wept and stumbled along just to see it, to be close to it, to touch it. The wonderful people of Poland had suffered greatly—and were still suffering—for their faith under the oppression of communism, and they were thrilled to see the symbol of their faith being carried through their country.

I stood at a village church for two hours while a steady flow of people came in and cried. A sweet woman who helped the priest couldn't speak. The priest told me the Nazis cut out her tongue when she was in Auschwitz. She cried and cried. The cross meant so much to her.

As I walked in a large open field, I could see people—thousands of people—coming across the field from every direction. They were running toward the cross. I couldn't believe my eyes. People left their work; they came on foot, on bicycles, in cars, on horses, and in wagons. They were crying, smiling, and laughing. It was awesome.

At the edge of a wheat field, where the nearest house was at least half a mile away and the closest town farther away than that, a huge crowd gathered. Cars and trucks stopped on both sides of the road. The traffic jam must have stretched for half a mile.

Crowds of people just kept coming as I walked through Poland. They filled churches and overflowed into the streets. Some drove many miles to see the man carrying the cross. People kissed the cross, and they kissed me! In the villages, people waited along the roadside for me to come to them. Word would spread, and masses of people would run across fields to see the cross.

Crafting a Cross

No one knows the exact measurements of the cross upon which Jesus died. Since I did not have a precise blueprint, I experimented over the years with how best to create a cross that can fit on a plane and then withstand the rigors of travel on the road.

I felt the wood should be strong enough to hold an adult man, so beams measuring four inches by four inches seemed about right. I estimated that a man's outstretched arms require a crossbeam about six feet wide. The height of the cross needs to accommodate a man at least six feet tall. About three additional feet of height are needed to set the cross upright into a hole. I figured that a three-foot gap between a person's feet and the ground would be appropriate. Therefore the upright beam of the cross needs to be about twelve feet in length.

So I designed a twelve-by-six-foot cross made of four-by-four-inch boards. At the crossbeam, a two-by-four-inch piece of wood is cut out of each beam to make it fit smoothly together. I used a metal plate to strengthen the crossbeam. The plate and the wood have holes drilled for a four-inch bolt to hold the crossbeam in place. This can also be unbolted for transport.

I ran into a problem taking the cross overseas. A twelve-foot cross was too long for checked baggage, so it had to be shipped airfreight on a separate flight. Unfortunately, there were many times I had trouble rendezvousing with the cross at my destination. It was lost twice, once for a month. So after six years, as I was about to go to the Pacific Islands in the summer of 1976, I cut the twelve-foot beam into two sections. Once I arrived at the airport, the pieces could be bolted together with a metal support on both sides, using the same type of bolts as the crossbeam.

Before the first cross-walk began on Christmas Day 1969, I had no idea how far and fast I could walk with the cross in a day. Several weeks before the walk was to begin, I went into the California desert to walk with the cross. During this test we realized that if it was not protected, the wood at the bottom of the cross would wear away at the rate of about an inch a day. Put wood against pavement or rock, and the wood will lose the battle every time! That is why I added a wheel at the base of the cross. After some experimentation, I determined that the best wheel is made from an inflatable tire about a foot in diameter. This size is common around the world, since it is used on tricycles. Plus, in many locations worldwide you can now get puncture-resistant tubes to prevent flats.

The unbolted cross conforms to all international baggage regulations. The three four-by-four-inch pieces of wood will fit inside a triple-ski bag. I have a canvas shop make the wheel end a little wider to fit the wheel.

The weight of the cross varies according to the type of wood used. The cross we carried across America weighs 110 pounds. The second cross, which I used until 1994, weighs 70 pounds. The cross I now carry weighs 45 pounds. I still have all three crosses.

Taking the Cross Off the Wall

The cross I made from wood, metal, and a wheel is not holy. But it does represent a truly holy event: the crucifixion of the Lord Jesus Christ! The cross is a dramatic symbol of that event. Yet while many people see crosses hanging on walls as decoration, my goal has been to get the cross off the wall and into people's minds and hearts, where they can understand and experience its message.

A large cross being carried makes an unforgettable impact on the mind of the person who sees it. Years later people still remember when and where they saw the cross being carried.

Symbols are very important in the Bible. In the Old Testament, events such as the Passover are full of symbols. In the New Testament, the bread and wine of Communion represent the body and blood of Jesus. Baptism and foot washing are other symbols used by believers. In the same way, the cross conveys a profound message when it is seen outside its usual context. Out on the road it touches the hearts of people who have worn a cross necklace for years. Churchgoers see so many crosses, they no longer make an impact; but if those same people leave church and see a person carrying a cross, they are shaken.

Some people have been critical of my walking with the cross around the world, saying, "Jesus has already done that." Yes, Jesus did carry the cross; but after a short distance Simon was compelled by the Roman soldiers to carry Jesus' cross. A sinner was qualified to carry the cross of Jesus, but he was not qualified to die on it for our sins.

Simon carried the cross to Calvary. Today we are to carry the cross to the world—maybe not in the literal sense, but as our Lord's caring representatives.

Jesus spoke often about the cross and its meaning:

> If anyone would come after me, he must deny himself and take up his cross and follow me. (Mark 8:34)

Anyone who does not carry his cross and follow me cannot be my disciple. (Luke14:27)

Anyone who does not take his cross and follow me is not worthy of me. (Matthew 10:38)

It is clear from these and other passages that followers of Jesus must be cross-carriers—probably not carriers of a physical cross, but cross-carriers nevertheless.

In Jesus' day the cross meant one thing: death. It was common for the Romans to use a cross as a way of suppressing occupied peoples. Jesus understood this before he was crucified. And his command that his disciples should carry their own cross implied that those who followed him were prepared to follow him to shame, reproach, and even death.

Jesus called me to carry his cross at five o'clock on a September morning in 1969. That's what I have been doing ever since. I carry a cross because he called me to do so and because that calling continues. I walk for Jesus because it is his will and plan for my life. That is why I am happy whatever happens. I walk with the cross in the rain, cold, or heat; when loved or hated; when welcomed or rejected; in honor or dishonor.

When I was carrying the cross in Switzerland, a man rushed up to me along a city street and said, "You look like the cross."

I was quite shocked and dismissed his words by saying, "I know I look a bit beat up and rough from the years of walking around the world."

"No, I don't mean that," he replied. "What I mean is that the cross fits you. If I took the cross and started carrying it, it would not look like me. But it does look like you."

After he left and I was walking down the road, I thought about what he said and came to realize what he meant. I began to weep, praying that my life would indeed look like the cross.

I pray that having walked in the shadow of the cross all these years I look more like Jesus today than when I began.

Chapter 4

Not If, but How

DARIEN JUNGLE

   As I lie in this hammock between two trees, my ears ring with the wild sounds of jungle life. The dark night is closing in on me, but the brightness of your light shines upon me.

   I can't sleep, Lord. I ache all over, and my arms sting from mosquito bites; I'm trembling in this cold.

   I'm stripped of dependence on anything but you, Jesus. You're showing me that prayer is more than speaking with you; it is living with you! I know you are walking with me, going with me through this struggle. It is so tough. But you know the way through this jungle.

Oh, hold me when I'm falling and lift me from the raging waters. I have nothing but you, and that is enough.

41

This is one of the
hardest struggles
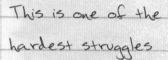
of my life; I don't even know if I'm going to make
it, but, in the name of Jesus, the Devil is not going
to kill me here. Jesus, if you want me to die, then
that's okay; but somehow, some way, you will lead
me through to
Colombia on the
other side. Glory.

One of the most important things I have learned in my journeys around the world with the cross is that I should focus not on *if*, but rather on *how*. *How* do I get the visa I need? *How* do I get into a country that is difficult to enter? *How* do I get across that river or up that mountain?

Those of us who want to go where Jesus sends us should remove from our vocabulary the small but potentially destructive word *if*, as I so keenly learned in the Darien Jungle of Panama and Colombia.

Facing Death in the Jungle

In 1979, ten years after God called me to carry the cross around the world, I found myself up against one of the world's deepest, darkest, most impenetrable jungles—the famous Darien Gap. As I carried the cross from Panama City, Panama, to Turbo, Colombia, I had to pass through rugged mountains, huge swamps, and thick forests where sunlight seldom reaches the ground.

The footing is often treacherous because of the heavy rainfall of about 180 inches a year. Conditions are hot and humid during the day; but, as I would discover, the nights get cold enough to need a blanket. There are deep, narrow rivers with rapids and waterfalls, steep cliffs covered in vines, and mile after mile of grass and thick brush. All kinds of fungi and diseases, including rabies, thrive in the Darien Jungle. And the region's insects, reptiles, and other animals are equally dangerous. Whether it's leeches, mosquitoes, ticks, spiders, scorpions, ants, panthers, wildcats, or snakes (there are three to watch out for: the six-foot coral snake; the fer-de-lance snake, which bites feet and ankles; and the bushmaster, which lives in trees and strikes the face and neck), there are many ways to die there.

It's no surprise that few people have traveled this stretch of land that joins the South American continent to the North American continent. But this jungle was where I had come to in my journey with the cross from Mexico to Colombia. God had called me two years earlier to carry the cross on foot from North America to South America.

I often travel with others to help me with supplies or to interpret, and this time two sturdy American men traveled with me. But as I would see, they focused more on *if* than on *how*.

Burdens and Blisters

Each of us carried a hundred-pound backpacks that held the gear we needed. My backpack was tied onto the back of the cross, which increased my load. With temperatures and humidity levels both hovering around 100, every step was hard work.

Conditions in the jungle grew worse each day, and my two partners suffered from sore backs and blisters. Five days into the journey, one of them said he was finished. Two days later, my other companion decided to drop out.

"Hey," I said, "we must do this together."

"But, Arthur, we can go around this area by boat or fly to Colombia," he replied. "We don't need to trudge through this jungle."

I was so numb from a combination of shock, pain, and aloneness that I didn't know what to say. After saying goodbye first to one friend and then the other, I wondered how they could do this to me. It was because they were thinking *if*, while I was thinking *how*.

Going It Alone

In this moment of crisis I had to decide which supplies I would need as I continued through the jungle alone. With tears streaming down my face, I chose my Swiss Army knife, a hammock, two rolls of Jesus stickers, my Bible, the clothes I was wearing, my passport, my money purse in a plastic waterproof bag, a tin of lemon drops, two canteens of water, and my machete.

I packed everything in the backpack, tied it onto the cross, and walked alone into the darkness of the jungle.

For weeks I walked up and down mountains and along riverbanks. I had to crawl up some of these mountains, pushing the cross a foot or two at a time. At other times the undergrowth was so thick that my arms became numb from swinging my machete. I was bleeding from several deep cuts. I was tired. I was wet. My back hurt. My feet were burning and bloody. But I went on.

I waded across as many as nine streams or rivers in a day, barely avoided going over cliffs and waterfalls, and grabbed onto vines to help me ascend and descend what seemed like a million valleys. I was particularly thankful when the vines didn't break. When they did break, I'd holler, "Jesus!" and push the cross one way while falling the other, praying I wouldn't land on a rock or a log.

Even sleep provided little relief. It was almost as difficult to sleep as it was to walk. I'd hang my hammock between two trees at night and lie shaking in the cold air. (To lessen the weight, I didn't take a blanket when I started out on my own.) In the morning I would whisper, *Jesus, I can start off again.*

During my weeks in the jungle I developed a taste for iguana meat. As the natives of this region do, I also carried iguana eggs with me to roast over a fire.

Day after day as I trudged forward, I asked God to give me strength to keep walking. One day I wrote in my journal: "My heart is so tender; my mind is tough; my body is in pain. But I'm going to make it by God's grace."

The People of the Jungle

I traveled day after day without seeing any sign of human life. But other days I knew I was getting closer to civilization, which happened one day when I came to a pigpen outside a village. I laid some boards that I found nearby across the top of the pen to make a simple bed. I called it the "Pig Hilton"! Those pigs never slept. It was grunt, grunt, grunt, bump, bump, bump all night long. Added to that was an awful smell.

Another day I emerged from the thick jungle into a village located at the side of a river.

At first everyone ran in fear. Then the people came toward me as I played with the small children. The houses in this village were erected on poles high above the ground. Neither the women nor the men wore much clothing. But that was okay. The thing that concerned me most was that I couldn't speak to them about Jesus in a way they could understand. When I spoke Spanish, they didn't respond. I wanted to share about Jesus, but how?

It was then that I felt the Lord leading me to present the gospel through dramatizing the crucifixion. Most of the villagers were sitting on the ground around me, while a few stood behind them. I took the cross and leaned it against one of the houses. I put up my hands to show them how the nails were driven through Jesus' hands and into the cross, but these people had no knowledge of nails—only cords.

As I tried to act out the crucifixion, I prayed: *O Lord, I don't mind struggling my way through this jungle, but I want these people to understand your love.* Tears flowed from my eyes as the desire to convey the message of Christ's sacrifice at Calvary overwhelmed me. I closed my eyes and prayed, *O Jesus, help them.*

As I opened my eyes, I saw that an older woman with no teeth had begun to cry. Soon the entire village was weeping. I went to the children and began saying, "Jesus, Jesus, Jesus," touching their beautiful little faces. Finally one of the children said, "Jesus," followed by many of the others. I pointed to the cross, then to heaven, then to my heart, and then to their hearts—each time saying, "Jesus."

Only God knows what the people in this village understood, but I later heard that missionaries who reached this village and spoke the language were told the people there had already heard of Jesus.

From that time on, drama became my main method of proclaiming the gospel when language posed a barrier.

(Note: This is quite different from the crucifixion reenactments carried out, most notably, in the Philippines, in which individuals are voluntarily nailed to wooden crosses every year on Good Friday. Such penitence is completely unnecessary and inappropriate, since Jesus Christ, the Son of God, is the only one who can be—and has been—crucified for the benefit of every human being. My dramatizations of the crucifixion are simple presentations in which it is obvious to the audience that I am playing the role of Jesus.)

A Meeting of Opposites

One day as I was cutting my way through the dense undergrowth

46

with my machete, miles and miles from civilization, I heard something that sounded like a chainsaw. I headed toward the sound and, during a pause in the commotion, called out, "Is anybody there?"

Surprisingly, an answer came back in English. "Yes!"

We cut toward each other in the jungle until I came face to face with a group of adventurers. They were traveling from the tip of South America to Alaska in two four-wheel-drive vehicles. They told me they were trying to become the first group to accomplish this feat.

This was a meeting of opposites.

Their group consisted of about seventeen white men accompanied by about twenty Indian porters.

I was on my own.

They looked like Indiana Jones.

I looked like someone who had been alone in the jungle for weeks—which I was.

They were dressed in nice clothes and carried the best and latest equipment, including hiking gear supplied by sponsoring companies and high-resolution cameras used to take photos for *National Geographic*.

I was dressed in sweaty rags of clothing and carried only my machete and a twelve-foot cross.

"What are you doing?" they asked in wonder.

"I'm carrying a cross," I said calmly.

"From where?"

"From Mexico to Colombia. Behind me is the trail I've cut."

They could hardly believe their eyes and ears. They invited me to join them for a meal, feeding me some of the best food I had eaten in weeks and filling my pockets with additional food. Plus they listened kindly as I told them about Jesus.

Much later, when I returned to my home in the United States, I received a letter from one of the men in the group. It included photos of some of the villages they went through as they proceeded in the same direction from which I had come. The photos featured near-naked villagers sporting the stickers I had given them that said, "Smile, God loves you!"

Reaching the Other Side

Finally, one month after heading into the Darien Jungle, I came out the other side at the wild town of Turbo, Colombia. I made quite an impression with my long hair and bushy beard, a machete swinging by my side, and the cross hanging on my shoulder.

Looking back on this experience, I'm reminded of these words of Jesus:

> As they were walking along the road, a man said to him, "I will follow you wherever you go."
>
> Jesus replied, "Foxes have holes and birds of the air have nests, but the Son of Man has no place to lay his head."
>
> He said to another man, "Follow me."
>
> But the man replied, "Lord, first let me go and bury my father."
>
> Jesus said to him, "Let the dead bury their own dead, but you go and proclaim the kingdom of God."
>
> Still another said, "I will follow you, Lord; but first let me go back and say good-by to my family."
>
> Jesus replied, "No one who puts his hand to the plow and looks back is fit for service in the kingdom of God." (Luke 9:57–62)

Jesus called me to the hot and muggy jungles of Latin America, and he led me through. Twenty years later he led me up and over one of the biggest and coldest mountains of the Far East.

From Pakistan to Afghanistan

The goal was to carry the cross from Pakistan to Afghanistan. The barrier that stood in our way was the historic Khyber Pass. This heavily armed route was not open for us to cross. But since the question was *how*—not *if*—we would proceed, we found another route near the remote and ancient town of Chitral.

The journey toward this higher pass started in a four-wheel-drive jeep Denise and I rode in for four hours near Tirich Mir, one of the highest mountains in the world. Our guide, a Muslim man named Syed, drove us up stone roads so narrow they could hold only one vehicle. These roads, cut out of the rocky cliffs, had no guardrails to protect us from the sheer drops that plunged hundreds of feet into a raging river.

When we reached an elevation of about nine thousand feet we stopped so I could assemble the cross and start walking. At the last village on the Pakistan side of the border we stopped, enjoyed hot tea, and spent the night before resuming our journey. We tried to share about Jesus, but our guide would not interpret the gospel message.

Up before dawn the next morning, I carried the cross while Denise road a donkey. But in time the way became so rocky and slippery the donkey would go no farther. Denise tried climbing the steep mountainside but could continue no longer. One of our guides said he would accompany her down the mountain to a camp where she could stay. I bid a tearful farewell. This would be our first night apart since we were married. Meanwhile, Syed and two other men climbed the mountain with me.

Soon we came to a major cliff. We took the cross apart so it could be hauled in three pieces. As we continued, the way grew steeper, more narrow, and more rugged. The cold wind penetrated to the bone as I shivered and shook. We found a place to camp for the night and ate a simple meal of roasted corn, wheat bread, and apricot seeds. Syed and I slept on a bed of rocks. I was cold and uncomfortable, but the night sky shone forth the glory of the Creator. Not even the painful rocky bed could keep my soul from rising above the discomfort to visit with God through the splendor of the night.

Early the next morning we continued up the slope. Each step was more difficult than the last, and each gain we made in elevation meant the oxygen we took into our weary bodies was thinner. There in the high Hindu Kush mountain range I learned that the only way I could make it was to pull my hat down over my eyes so I could see only about ten steps in front of me. I gave everything I had to complete those ten steps. Then I would lift my head so I could see ten more steps. That was how we continued over boulders and across a massive glacier.

At one point I was so exhausted I cried out to God: *I'm too tired, too exhausted to pray. I can't even think clearly. Only you can get me up there! You know all my needs. I'll just repeat the name of Jesus, and you take care of me. You can give me pure oxygen!* I did not experience any headaches or major bouts of nausea for the rest of the climb.

After more sliding, stumbling, and struggling we made it to the top of Bronzal Pass at 18,200 feet, which is the highest I have gone in my journeys with the cross. I quickly laid the three pieces of the cross out and bolted them together. Then lying face down on the ground so that my body straddled the border between Pakistan and Afghanistan, I prayed. I prayed for peace, the blessings of God, and love to fill every heart. Then I raised the cross upright and looked at the two beautiful glaciers we had walked across. I also gazed at the 25,000-foot mountain, Tirich Mir, which towered over us. I was so excited. This was one of the most glorious moments of my life.

It had taken us eight hours to reach the summit. After enjoying the view, we walked a short distance down the other side of the mountain into Afghanistan. The men helped me with the cross in case the cold, wild wind blew me over. We climbed back to the summit. Now the cross had been in Afghanistan!

I looked at Syed and the other members of our team with tears in my eyes as I prayed for each of them and their families. These Muslim men put their lives in danger and faced death to help me take the cross to the top of this mountain. They never complained or turned back.

I'll never forget what Syed told me when I thanked him: "It's my moral responsibility to help you. You are on a mission from God to carry the cross in every nation. It's my moral responsibility to help you accomplish this for God. I gave my word; I would never consider changing it!"

Syed interpreted to the two porters as I shared the message of the cross. All three of them prayed and welcomed Jesus into their lives on the mountain that day.

The Journey Back

After resting for about an hour, we began the return trip back down to our starting point in Pakistan. You might think this would be easier, but the descent was more dangerous than the ascent. The weight of the cross, which we had again taken apart so it could be carried in three pieces, pushed us down the sliding rocks. As we descended, my legs felt weak and rubbery. The other men had to support me to keep me from sliding down the mountain.

Before dark we made it back to the camp where Denise was staying. From a distance I could see her waving in the valley below. When I finally got to her, just as darkness fell, I literally fell into her arms. We fell asleep thanking God for his great mercy, grace, and safety.

The next morning we continued our return journey to Chitral, Pakistan. Denise rode a donkey, and I walked alongside her as we set off down the valley. First we passed through pastures of green grass by streams, then cornfields located in small patches of the canyon, and then wheat in areas wide enough to plant a small field. We continued along steep cliffs and over raging waters, which we crossed with the help of rope-and-stone bridges.

We slept again in Chitral, but our hearts were still on the mountain that towered above us. As Denise and I talked about this journey, we thought about something Syed said to us. During one of the trip's difficult moments, he looked at us and said, *"It's only a challenge!"*

The Difference between No and Go

At the beginning of this chapter I talked about the word *if.* Another member of my list of least-favorite words is the small word *no.* Only one letter is different between the words *no* and *go,* but what a difference of meaning is conveyed.

Over the years I have encountered many challenges. My goal, however, has been not to allow myself to be defeated, but rather to keep seeking the way forward—whether it is straight ahead or up or under or around. First I try one thing and then another as I follow Jesus' leading. Then, when the way opens before me, I rush through.

When Jesus calls you to follow him, or when he gives you an assignment to fulfill, I pray you will focus not on *if*, but on *how*—because I believe that, with God's grace, you will achieve amazing things.

Chapter 5

Family Life on the Road

DENISE IN IRAN

Wow, what a radical and awesome woman I am married to. Today Denise flung off her Islamic headscarf and put on her hat! With a defiant smile she said to me, "I'm going to wear my hat today!"

I sat in stunned silence.

She is no fool; she knows the possible consequences. I wondered where we would be tonight: dead, imprisoned, or celebrating.

Denise got more attention today in Iran than the cross and me. I prayed for her, and Jesus

gave her mercy and protection. The people loved her. I never know what she might do next! But,

Lord, I am so blessed to be loved by her and to be able to love her. She is such a free spirit in Jesus.

Jesus, you broke traditions and norms; what a great example to follow.

God, you have been so good to us. Even walking through the city market with the cross with Denise wearing her hat, you blessed us and protected us. Here in this ancient and historic land we lift the cross and Jesus up. We love you, Lord, and thanks for giving us the opportunity to share with others your life and salvation.

Keep us, Lord, in the palm of your hand.

JOEL AND JOSHUA
in Jordan

I felt totally helpless looking at Joshua about to pass out, and I was too weak and dizzy to help. But you gave us a little shade under that tree. In a parched and dry land water came forth in the form of ice! Joel came bearing a miracle! Oh my Lord, thank you for the water.

I don't know who can understand the feeling of leading my two sons through the desert with only a cross and our backpacks. But few can know the bond of love and unity that comes when walking in the valley of the shadow of death

I am so proud of my sons. I pray they live long enough to become adults. They have faced so much with me on the roads of the world, and I love them dearly. Thank you, Jesus.

God created the earth and all that is in it and "saw that it was good." Yet it did not stay that way. How sad. Often some things in life do not turn out as we dreamed they would. This happened in one important area of my life.

After many years of struggles, discussions, and prayers, my first wife and I agreed to officially end our marriage. We both vowed to God we would not discuss our personal difficulties with other people. We left all our judgments and hurts at the feet of Jesus, where they belong, freeing us to face the future.

I have chosen to focus on the blessing of the six wonderful children God gave us. As I write this, I am also the grandfather of ten grandchildren. How glorious.

The presence, strength, and love of Jesus were and are sufficient to meet every need. I remember many months when my Bible was my pillow at night. Through it all Jesus led so gently, as he stripped, washed, cleansed, healed, empowered, blessed, and filled my life.

Divorce is not the result of success, but of failure. We both tried but failed. I'm so grateful for God's grace and its ability to overshadow our sins and failures. The cross provides the power to forgive and restore, not only in terms of salvation but also in every area of our lives.

I am grateful for the wonderful people who, over the years, have joined with me to accomplish God's purpose for my life. The team has come together naturally, and I have been so blessed to receive the help they have given me.

Marrying Denise has been yet another example of God's grace and kindness to me. She has helped me continue pursuing God's calling for my life. We married in 1990, and during the next decade we walked in about sixteen or seventeen nations a year.

Typically Denise dropped me off with the cross at a given point, drove ahead in our Land Rover, and waited for me. We would set up for the night in one of a number of settings. Some places were safe and comfortable, while many were not. But Denise never complained, and she met every circumstance and challenge right by my side.

I want you to know, in Denise's own words, what this journey has been like from her perspective.

Denise's Story

A Heart for Jesus and for Missions

I grew up in England and was educated at an all-girls school in a Catholic convent. From the time I was a little girl I loved hearing stories about Jesus. But I did not know him personally.

As I grew up, matters of spirituality consumed me, and I was drawn to the occult and many New Age beliefs. But my life was empty and filled with despair. In July 1983 I was sitting cross-legged in the grass at Wimbledon Common. "God if there is more to you than I have ever been told, then show me now—or I will end my life," I cried aloud. I was sobbing and rocking back and forth with my head in my hands.

A woman approached me tentatively and asked, "Are you all right?"

"No, I'm not!" I cried back to her.

This dear African woman, Yvonne, introduced me to her husband, and they told me about Jesus—that he was real and that I could know him. I was absolutely thrilled to hear this, and I accepted Jesus into my life that moment.

My life was transformed. After so many years of wandering in darkness, I was now in the light. The love of Jesus infused my soul, and I felt a deep sense of lasting joy that is still with me today.

My desire was to be a missionary, but because I didn't have a Bible school education, I was rejected. I was so disappointed. I lived in a Christian community that took in people from different ethnic groups. Many were from Africa, Asia, or Europe. I would have a dream of traveling to Japan to tell people about Jesus and then another dream of going to India to tell people *there* about Jesus. I couldn't make up my mind where God was leading me. I thought I was being indecisive.

I wanted to go to the entire world, but I ended up with a job in a large and prestigious British company. My training there prepared me to deal with persons from all walks of life. Both ordinary people and important dignitaries came through our office, and I learned to work with all of them. I learned how to be organized and to handle many details simultaneously.

Little did I know what God had in store for me—Arthur Blessitt!

Arthur came into my life, and my longing to be a missionary was soon to be realized. I would be traveling the world for the rest of my life, taking care of details and organizing many aspects of our travels. God prepared me for this most unusual life that Arthur and I live.

The Wedding with the Cross

Arthur and I married in London in June 1990. The church was lovely, and many of my family and friends were there to celebrate with us.

We made a joint vow that day to God and to each other to carry the cross in every nation by the year 2000. That may be considered an unusual part of a wedding ceremony, but it meant so much to us. "It's my calling too," I often explained when people asked what I thought of Arthur's life calling.

Arthur's cross stood behind the altar and could easily have been mistaken for one of the church's fixtures. Then, as the ceremony ended, Arthur walked behind the altar and grabbed the cross so he could carry it down the aisle with us. I smiled and thought to myself, *My dear friends and relatives probably think he is tearing the church apart!*

The three of us—the cross, Arthur, and I—walked down the aisle. We've been doing that ever since: Arthur walking with the cross on one side and me on the other.

Our life of adventure, following Jesus, had begun. Arthur and I work together beautifully. It's so exciting and rewarding to not only do what you are called to do and love but also do it with the person you love. I am deeply blessed!

Rising above Fear

Because Arthur and I are often in dangerous situations, people frequently ask me, "How do you cope with fear?"

All I have to do is think about my experience at Wimbledon Common. I didn't see Yvonne again for almost a year. But at a meeting with some friends, I noticed this familiar-looking African woman. It was Yvonne!

Yvonne told me something that day that changed me. She had been afraid to approach me when she saw me rocking back and forth there in the grass. My behavior made her think I was sniffing glue. My head was down, my hands were covering my mouth and nose, and I was sobbing and rocking. Because of so many glue sniffers in London at the time, she assumed I was high and might respond with anger if approached. But rather than giving in to fear, she came up to me.

Imagine what might have happened to me if Yvonne had given in to her fear. The moment I heard Yvonne share her story, I promised God I would never let fear stop me from telling someone about Jesus. And God has made me live that promise. There is a world full of people living in the kind of darkness I was in that day at Wimbledon Common. Jesus takes care of my fear; I trust him and go forward.

A Somali Fighter Woman

There are a few stories about me that Arthur loves because he thinks they reflect who I am as we travel with the cross. Here's one of them.

We were trying to get into Somalia, and the only way was to fly into Dubai in the United Arab Emirates (U.A.E.) and make a connection there. Because I was a British citizen, I had no trouble getting into Dubai, but Arthur needed a visa and didn't have one. The airport authorities in Dubai agreed to let him into the airport, but they kept his passport.

A few days later when the flight to Somalia was due to leave from another airport in the U.A.E., the authorities refused to give Arthur's passport back to him. Arthur was sitting on a bench outside the airport concourse with his head in his hands. So I went to the parking lot and met the two Somali men who were to assist us with the trip to Somalia. I asked the men, as they sat in their van, to speak to the authorities to help Arthur get his passport so we could leave the airport. They didn't move to help, and I thought they were getting ready to drive off.

I ran in front of the van and planted my feet firmly in front of their vehicle. I stared at them, and they knew I was *not* going to move. Finally one of the men changed his mind and hopped out of the van. "Right!" he said, as he headed into the airport. I motioned to Arthur and said, "Follow me!"

The man succeeded in getting Arthur's passport returned to him. But then he and the other Somalian started to leave us stranded at the airport. I stopped them and told them that they had to give us a ride into town. God gave us favor. We got into the back of the van, and the driver took off.

One of the men turned to Arthur and said, "Sir, I like your wife. She not like white Western woman. She Somali fighter woman!"

The Somali Fighter Woman in Iran

"It was nothing less than an act of revolution. The woman was wearing a hat."

That was the first sentence in an article written by Elaine Sciolino in the *New York Times* February 8, 1998.

It was January 1998, and we were in Iran, where Arthur was carrying the cross. To combat the cold, the buildings were heated to a steamy temperature. As a woman visiting that country, I was to dress fully covered and was not even allowed to take off my coat.

We were going on a day tour to view some ancient monuments, and I decided to wear a hat—even though women in Iran had not been permitted to wear hats that revealed any part of their hair since shortly after the revolution nineteen years earlier. A hat would be cooler than the scarves I'd been wearing. It was also my bit for women's emancipation in Iran.

At the ancient site, a woman stared at me. She approached Arthur and asked, "Who is she?"

"That's my wife," he replied. "Who are you?"

She told Arthur she was a writer for the *New York Times* and asked if she could talk to me. As we talked, she expressed her surprise that I was wearing a hat rather than a headscarf and that I had not been arrested! I told her, "I know I'm only one woman, but God is with me. I believe I have God's protection."

She had to admit that I had God's protection!

I know that God won't let anything happen to me until he has fulfilled his purpose for me. God stirs my spirit and gives me boldness and favor, and I simply say, *Lord, your will be done.*

A Very Special Blessing

As Arthur and I travel the world, I am so touched by the children we see and meet. I loved to be with them, hug them, and tell them about Jesus.

Arthur has six children, and in 1998 he and I started talking about having a child of our own. I had just fallen in love with so many children from many countries. It seemed so natural when God led us to adopt Sophia from another nation. We were thrilled and blessed beyond belief.

Sophia joined us as an infant and has traveled with us from the beginning. Life on the road is normal for her. She has to be one of the most well-traveled four-year-olds in the world, and she loves to meet children in different countries.

We have tried to teach Sophia to appreciate how much she has and to realize that so many children have so little. Recently she was with us on some islands in the Indian Ocean. We bought gifts for the children, and Sophia distributed them to a roomful of excited little ones. It was wonderful to see her experience the joy of giving.

Now that Denise has told some of her story, let me introduce you to my son Joel, who is my second-oldest child and is forty-two years old. Joel is on the staff of the church where we worship and have our office. He will share what it was like to grow up in a family in which his father carried a cross around the world.

Joel's Story

All six of us kids traveled with Dad. We trekked throughout the world together and were homeschooled. It didn't seem unusual, because that was the life we knew.

When I was about four or five, we made our first trip overseas. We traveled in Africa, England, Spain, and Portugal. That was the first time I realized that we lived differently from most people. We made new friends everywhere we went, but I saw that they lived in one place and didn't travel around as we did. I actually preferred our life; and when we did spend about a year in England, I missed being on the road.

Seeing God Provide

Dad has already filled books with ways God has worked in his life and in ours, but one trip stands out in my mind. My brother Josh and I went with Dad on a trip through Jordan. I was about thirteen at the time and excited to be in on this adventure. We were traveling on foot, with no vehicle dropping us off and driving ahead to pick us up. Our only belongings were in a backpack that hung on the cross.

We were walking in 115-degree heat in a valley between Jordan and Israel when we ran into trouble: we ran out of water. There was no one around and no shade. Dad and Josh both started to show signs of dehydration. They felt faint, and our plan to move forward until we found water wasn't working. Just when I thought they both might collapse, we saw a grove of trees. We managed to get there, and Dad and Josh gratefully fell down in the shade.

I was still doing okay, but I knew I had to find help. I went to the nearby road and tried to flag down passing vehicles. It was the middle of Ramadan, the month in which Muslims don't carry food or water because they are fasting. So even if people wanted to help, they had no water with them.

Finally one car stopped that had a cooler of ice. Those people may have been cheating a little on their fast, but I was so grateful. I held out my shirt, filled it full of ice cubes, and ran back to Dad and Josh. They sucked on the ice and put some on their heads. Soon they were all right, and we were able to go on, praising God for his provision.

Some Strange Things along the Way

Eating was often an adventure in itself. I think the strangest thing I ever ate was in the Bahamas: we were served fish and given the "honor" of eating the eyeballs! I ate them to be polite, but it wasn't pleasant. There were a lot of times in Asia I had no idea what I was eating. But I never got sick.

The strangest thing I ever saw occurred in Spain when Dad was preaching at an outside rally. All of a sudden riot police came storming into the crowd, beating everyone to the ground. I was thrown down, and other people fell on top of me. I was scared and didn't know what had happened. In the middle of the chaos, someone pulled me away from the mob. All I could see as I was being taken away was the cross falling down. I thought my dad was being killed.

Missionaries we knew were protecting me, and I ended up in a church where people being released from jail were gathering. Dad walked in and hugged me! He was safe, and even the cross was okay. The riot police had put it back up and were guarding it.

A Tribute

My dad is the most faithful follower of Jesus I have ever known. He is truly determined to do what God is telling him to do. I can say that because I have walked with him for thousands of miles, and now, as an adult, I watch him just keep on going. I wish I were half as committed as he is. I know of no one who has reached more individuals with the love of Jesus than Dad. He is amazing!

The Journey Continues

There are so many family members and other people who have helped me accomplish my life's purpose. I am grateful to God for each of them.

Denise, Sophia, and I are the major team travelers now. Denise still drives and cooks, and now she takes care of Sophia too. I still carry the cross. We are not alone. We have each other; and always, always we have Jesus. Praise his name!

Chapter 6

The Roar of the Crowds, the Silence of the Jail Cell

I have learned to be content whatever the circumstances. I know what it is to be in need, and I know what it is to have plenty. I have learned the secret of being content in any and every situation, whether well fed or hungry, whether living in plenty or in want. I can do everything through him who gives me strength.
—Philippians 4:11–13

KGB IN RUSSIA

It's Denise and me in a huge mess and battle again. It was an all-day struggle against the forces of evil and communism. Now it's night; and, Jesus, we made it through the day. You gave us the strength to stand strong and pray as voices were yelling at us and fingers were waved in our faces. We gripped each other's hands; but you, God, held us in your hand.

And now tonight as we lie in our Land Rover, it is quiet in these mountains.

We endured reproach; we shared about you and your love. You sent us a man to be our

deliverer. It was like
he was born to be
there, just to help us at
that time. This is not
just a daily battle but
almost an hourly battle.
We cling to you and feel
so close to you. Yet we are so far away from the
world we have known. Somehow we will make it.

I could not have made it without Denise. Thank
you, Jesus, for her. We love you, and we have the
joy of another
day before us . . .
come what may.

The "Washington for Jesus" rally in April 1980 was a real high point for me. A huge crowd—perhaps half-a-million people—gathered in the nation's capital to pray, sing, and listen to speakers such as Pat Robertson, Jerry Falwell, and Bill Bright. I had carried the cross from Virginia Beach to Washington, where I planned to participate in the rally just like thousands of others. But Robertson, host of *The 700 Club* TV program, had a different idea.

Pat rushed over to me and grabbed my arm. "The cross leads the way in our Jesus march," he said.

"But I'm not on the program," I replied. "I wasn't planning to be in the front."

"We go!" he said, brushing aside my hesitancy. "I marched when I was a marine. Now I want to march beside you."

With live TV beaming the march to millions of people around the nation and the world, Pat and I, followed by tens of thousands of people, made a large loop around the area. It was awesome to see well-known Christian leaders joining average Americans as we walked through the capital with the cross.

As our procession circled back toward the rally's stage area, singers Dottie and Reba Rambo sang "I Will Glory in the Cross." It was thrilling to see people focusing not on politicians or issues, but on the cross. After all, the apostle Paul once said, "God forbid that I should boast except in the cross of our Lord Jesus Christ" (Galatians 6:14 NKJV).

The rally was about to begin. I was putting the cross behind the stage area when Paul Crouch, the founder and president of the Trinity Broadcasting Network, came up to me and looked me in the eyes. "Take the cross up on the stage, Arthur," he said.

I stared at him. I hadn't planned to be on the stage—and I wasn't exactly dressed for the occasion. I was wearing blue jeans and a Levi shirt, while the other men on the program were wearing suits and ties. I was dressed casually because I had been walking with the cross.

"I'll take responsibility for this," Paul said, with a reassuring look on his face. "Don't be afraid to be up front after all these years you have been carrying the cross around the world."

Paul and I climbed the steps to the stage, where I raised the cross upright to its full twelve-foot height. As I did so, the entire crowd exploded with shouts of praise.

I didn't have a microphone to address the crowd, so I said to the Lord: "Jesus, I pray you are pleased as we glory in you and your cross."

Then Paul told me that his comments would be shorter than planned, and he asked me to address the crowd when he finished. I was not expecting this, but I was ready. I had carried the cross alone around the world; now I welcomed the chance to speak about the cross to this huge crowd.

The next thing I knew, Paul was introducing me. "There is someone here who is not on the program, but I feel he should say something to you. His name is Arthur Blessitt, and he has carried this cross around the world."

People stood on their feet and cheered as I came forward. In return, I shouted: "Give me a J!"

The crowd roared back: "J!"

"Give me an E!"

"E!"

"Give me an S!"

"S!"

"Give me a U!"

"U!"

"Give me an S!"

"S!"

"What does that spell?"

"JESUS!"

Then I looked at the crowd, and these words spilled out of me: "There is a lost world around us. As you leave here today, tell someone about Jesus on your way home."

Then I referred to the Old Testament prophet Isaiah. "God is asking us the same question he asked Isaiah: 'Whom shall I send? And who will go for us?' And Isaiah answered, 'Here am I, Lord. Send me!' Say it with me now, everyone: 'Here am I, Lord. Send me!'"

The crowd roared back: "Here am I, Lord. Send me!"

It was a wonderful and glorious surprise to speak to this

crowd—something I will never forget. But there are other times when no crowds are listening to me speak or cheering as I walk with the cross.

Being Triumphant in Tough Times

I've had many unforgettable experiences, such as speaking to half-a-million people at that rally in Washington and to half-a-million music fans at the 1970 Atlanta International Pop Festival. But most of the time I am alone, walking mile after mile with no one to cheer me or even see me. And there have been twenty-four times when I was arrested or thrown into jail.

My first run-in with the police happened in Jackson, Mississippi, in the early 1960s. A college kid at the time, I held a black man's hand as I prayed with him on the street to receive Jesus. I didn't know that was against the law.

Of all my jail experiences, the worst took place in Concord, New Hampshire, in 1976. I was carrying the cross with my two oldest children, Gina (who was twelve) and Joel (who was ten). Two police officers drove up in a patrol car and arrested me for soliciting money, which I have never done in my life. They threw down the cross, hand-cuffed me, and took me to jail—leaving Gina and Joel on the street alone. Because it was Friday afternoon, I had to wait until Monday to appear in court. The judge threw out the case and lectured the police officers who arrested me about their stupid actions.

I have carried the cross in 315 countries and island groups. In most of these nations I have had great experiences, although 52 of these countries were at war. I have seen beautiful places and wonderful people, but I have also seen horrors and tragedies. I faced a firing squad in Nicaragua; I was almost stoned and beaten in Morocco; I was attacked by police in Spain; a Los Angeles police officer tried to choke me in Hollywood; I survived an angry man's pistol attack in Orlando, Florida; a man in Birdseye, Indiana, tried to burn the cross; and a man in Nigeria broke the cross.

I have enjoyed some wonderful meals, including freshwater shrimp in El Salvador and fresh salmon in Finland. I have also eaten some stomach-churning concoctions, including squid in ink (Spain), monkey leg (Africa), and rat soup (Belize).

I have been warmly received in some places (for example, Papua New Guinea, Poland, Spain, India, Lithuania, Kiribati, Solomon Islands, Vanuatu, and central Africa), and I have been coldly rejected in others (for example, New York City, Montreal, and Sydney). And speaking of "warmly" and "coldly," I have carried the cross through the Jordan Valley in Israel when the temperature was 135 degrees, and I have carried the cross in Nova Scotia when the temperature was 20 degrees below zero.

Why do I tell you all this? Because of a simple lesson I learned long ago that has stuck with me all these years: We need to follow God's call, regardless of whether people love us or hate us.

God's call is not conditional. It doesn't depend on favorable conditions, warm weather, or good moods. When God calls us to do something, may we be like the apostle Paul—who said yes to such divine assignments, knowing God would help him learn to be content, no matter what circumstances he faced.

The Cross Meets a Coup in Burundi

When Denise and I traveled to the central African nation of Burundi in 1996, we had no idea we would walk into a military coup.

We arrived in the capital city of Bujumbura amid hostile tension between the Hutu and Tutsi tribes. I was glad we could carry the cross through the center of town during such a difficult time, but most of the people we saw seemed frightened. Then a convoy of army trucks came our way. The people really backed away from us as the soldiers jumped out of their trucks and came toward us, pointing to the trucks to indicate we should get in.

I didn't want to be separated from the cross. As long as we had the cross, it was clear what we were doing; without the cross we were just tourists. I lifted the cross and shoved it onto the back of one of the trucks. The soldiers didn't like this and screamed, "No!" Then I leaped onto the back of the truck and helped Denise climb up. We sat with our arms around the cross.

Denise and I prayed as the convoy started moving. We were taken to a military compound on the outskirts of the city. Troops were everywhere and seemed ready to move out for an imminent battle. The soldiers motioned for us to get off the truck. Taking the cross with us, we were ushered into a small office where we were interrogated in French. Neither Denise nor I understood French, which made the officers quite angry.

One of the things I have learned from the many times I have been arrested and interrogated around the world is to hang on. If you hold out long enough, you will eventually be passed to a more senior officer. "These men are not the decision makers," I told Denise. "They won't do anything without permission from their commander."

After a while we were taken to a nice office area. A man in a uniform decorated with many medals warmly greeted us in English and shook our hands. "Don't you know it's dangerous here?" he asked.

"Yes," I replied. "But the cross is needed in the places of suffering and death and hurt."

I began telling him about our walk with the cross and showing him photos of me with various world leaders. He seemed to enjoy this, but he remained concerned about our presence in Burundi.

"I also believe in Jesus," he said. "But we have a war to fight. Why are you here now?"

"Well, we are carrying the cross in every nation," I explained, "and this is one of the nations where we have never carried the cross. Since we're on a trip to Africa now, we feel this is the time to be here. War or peace, our mission is the same."

The commander seemed deeply moved. He said we were free to go but warned us again of the dangers we faced.

"My men will drive you to your hotel," he said.

"That's very kind of you," I replied. "But we would rather carry the cross back."

After praying for him and for peace in Burundi, that's exactly what we did—walk out of the compound and through the streets of the city.

Back at the hotel later that day, we noticed the streets were empty except for police and army vehicles. We soon learned why.

The president of Burundi had just been overthrown in a military coup.

We were confined to our hotel for several days, but as soon as the curfew was lifted, we again took the cross into the streets. Earlier, people seemed aloof or afraid, but now they greeted us and welcomed the cross.

I told one of the journalists in the hotel about the sudden change in reception. He explained to me the reason. The deposed president had announced on radio and television that the only thing that would persuade him to leave office would be the coming of Jesus. The people believed our carrying the cross was a sign that had happened! The unpopular president fled to the U.S. embassy, and the army took over. We were treated like heroes and VIPs during the rest of our visit.

One officer approached us and asked what was in the cross. "It's only wood," I told him.

He looked at me and said, "No, there is power in that cross!"

When our adventure in Burundi was over, I complimented Denise on her bravery and calm demeanor. She replied that while she may have *looked* calm, internally she was terrified.

"When we were put on the truck, we didn't know what the soldiers were going to do to us. My heart was pounding so loudly I felt certain everyone would hear it. But when I get in frightening situations like that, I pray and cry out in prayer: 'O Jesus, help me!' Despite the terrifying feelings and the sound of my heart pounding in my chest, I've always known that God is in control. No matter how fearful I feel, I know God is there with us."

Our Time with the KGB

How many movies have you seen or books have you read about the KGB, Russia's notorious Committee for State Security? Denise and I had our own encounter with the KGB while we carried the cross through the area once known as the Union of Soviet Socialist Republics. We traveled through this region in 1992, soon after all the former Soviet republics formed independent countries. Perhaps that made the KGB officials more edgy.

When Denise and I arrived at a roadblock in the Asian country of Uzbekistan, the police wanted to check our papers. We had passports and other papers, but no visa. They demanded a visa. Soon other officers arrived, and in moments police cars surrounded our vehicle. The cars escorted us to the police headquarters, where we were taken into a large room with a long table for a lengthy interrogation.

Denise and I sat on one side of the table while several people sat across from us, some in uniforms and others in plain clothes. A local schoolteacher who taught English interpreted the questions and our answers.

"Why are you here?"

"How did you get into this country?"

"Are you spies?"

"Whom do you know in this country?"

"Where did you get your money?"

We tried to explain, showing them the map we used traveling through several thousand miles of the former USSR. They were not impressed.

"How did you get through all the borders?" they asked.

"Jesus did it," we said. That really seemed to send them into a rage.

The session continued for several more hours. Then a military officer who seemed to be of a higher rank than many of the others came in to listen to the interrogation. Soon he came over and sat beside me, saying nothing. As the others pressed us for more answers, I noticed the officer reach into his shirt pocket to pull out something I couldn't see. A moment later I saw in the palm of his hand an icon of the Virgin Mary with the infant Jesus. The other people in the room couldn't see this, but I certainly did. Although he didn't look at me, I felt he was trying to let me know he was a believer in Jesus.

The interrogation continued, and then this officer stood up and said something to the others. They all left the room. The interpreter told us the officer was inviting us to have lunch with him. There was no way to tell what was really happening, so I told the interpreter we would accept. I looked at Denise and said, "Let's go."

We were taken to a black limousine and put in the back seat. In the front seat sat the driver and the officer. No one said a word to us as we drove down the road, escorted by a number of police cars in front and behind us.

We stopped in front of a restaurant. The officer said something to the driver, who got out and joined the people who had come in the other cars. Then the officer turned to face Denise and me. As he did so, he held the icon in his hand.

"I want to give this to you," he said in perfect English. "This is the only thing I have from my mother, who loved Jesus and taught me to love him also. Before she died, she gave this to me, and every day I carry it in my shirt over my heart. Like you, I believe in Jesus. Thank you for what you are doing. Keep it up. We need it."

"Thank you," I said. "We will."

"When we have lunch together, I will not speak English," the officer said. "Afterward the KGB will come and take you away. They will question you and threaten you, but do not fear. You will be released before nightfall. Once you are released, drive to the border. When the other officers in the chain of command contact me, I will pardon you and set you free. You will not see me again after our lunch, but I will be checking to make sure everything works out."

Before he turned to get out of the car, he looked at us and said, "God bless you." Tears filled his eyes.

After lunch we never saw him again. Sure enough, KGB officials took us to a different location and interrogated us for a few more hours. They threatened us, shouted at us, and did almost everything but hit us. As the interrogation continued, we began wondering about the promise made to us by the officer. *What would happen to us? Where would we be tonight?*

Suddenly a high-ranking KGB official told us that the officer with whom we shared lunch had forgiven our many great offenses. "You are free to go!" he said.

The officials took us back to our Land Rover, which still had the cross tied to its side. We got in and drove into the night, crossing the border out of Uzbekistan and away from these KGB men.

Five years later we received a letter from the officer who arranged our release. It was now safe for him to contact us. He sent his blessings along with a photo that showed the three of us outside the restaurant where we had lunch together that day.

Faithful, No Matter What

My goal in sharing these stories with you is not to make Denise and me look special or superhuman. Rather, my intent is to encourage you to stay focused on Jesus and remain faithful to the calling he has given you, no matter what other people say or do.

Some of the earliest followers of Jesus spent time in jail. But even though people may arrest us and throw us in jail, they will never be able to arrest our faith, our zeal, or our love for God and for others.

Some individuals are overly sensitive to the critical things others say. But God has shown me that when we learn to receive criticism and praise with the same detached attitude we are then set free from the power of public opinion. We are no longer held captive to what other people think, do, or say.

My desire is to *act* on what Jesus tells me to do, not *react* to other people. Like Paul says in Philippians 4:12, "I have learned the secret of being content in any and every situation, whether well fed or hungry, whether living in plenty or in want."

A classic Christian song perfectly captures this concept:

> Though none go with me, still I will follow;
> Though none go with me, still I will follow;
> Though none go with me, still I will follow;
> No turning back, no turning back.

My prayer for you is that as you follow Jesus you will remain faithful, no matter what.

Chapter 7

Daily News

Tuesday, August 17, 1982

Missionaries in war zone

Arthur Blessitt and his son, carrying crosses on their backs, pass in front of Israeli troop carriers near Green Line that separates East and West Beirut. The Blessitts have crossed to Palestinian-controlled western sector of the city on a mission of peace, with the father trying to talk people into "turning on to Jesus." Related story in section 1, page 3.

Ambassadors of <u>Peace</u> in a World of <u>War</u>

Blessed are the peacemakers, for they will be called sons of God.
—Matthew 5:9

ARAFAT—BEIRUT

I can't sleep tonight as bombs explode and guns fire all around us. But Joshua is asleep. We've had nothing to eat and I'm so hungry. Looking back on this day I tremble.

I walked through a minefield and a battlefield with my young son. The way you kept Joshua safe reminded me of the way you kept Isaac safe when Abraham led him up the mountain to die. No matter how much fear I felt today, I knew that not trying would be worse than dying. I cannot live with having stopped short of doing what you tell me to do, Lord. I felt almost numb as we walked through the fighting

armies, but Joshua
was so strong and
had the glory of
the Lord on his
face.

Oh Jesus, you
led us right into the
arms of Yasser Arafat and had us pray for him.

Joshua and I held our crosses with Arafat
between us. I know many will criticize us for praying
with him and hugging him; but, Jesus, you let the
sinner touch you, hold you, and kiss you. You led us
from Sweden to West Beirut to pray for Arafat,
and I am still shaking.

The cross
and I are
supposed to be
in the center
of conflict and
need, where
life and death
are raging. It

forces me to deny myself and do your will. I suppress all my emotions, fears, desires, and dreams and step out into the madness with a smile, peace, and Jesus.

   This was truly church today. Pews were foxholes with people huddled behind barricades; the lights were bombs bursting; the choir was the sound of explosions with the screams of the wounded and dying. The sanctuary was full of tracer bullets, screeching rockets, and men shouting. But everyone was interested and welcomed us, the cross, and Jesus!

In the summer of 1980 I was in predominantly Muslim West Beirut, Lebanon, with the cross. The Palestinians and Israelis, as usual, were fighting for territory and autonomy. I had been praying that God would give me the opportunity to meet a man who, depending on your point of view, was either {a) a hero, patriot, and liberator respected by millions of people throughout the world or {b) the world's most notorious terrorist. Before arriving there, I heard many people say many things about this man.

About midnight, some armed men suddenly awakened me. "Yasser Arafat wants to see you," they said.

I dressed quickly and went with the men in their car, which raced without headlights through the battle-strewn streets of Beirut. Soon I was looking into the eyes of the chairman of the Palestinian Liberation Organization, or PLO. As I looked at this small, energetic man wearing a traditional Palestinian head wrap and sporting a pistol strapped to his hip, I saw someone whose eyes were alive and sparkling.

"Well," I said, smiling, "I guess it's one fanatic meeting another!"

He reached out his arms and hugged me, and we exchanged kisses in the traditional Arab custom.

Here we were, two radicals seeking to make people free. One had a cross and the other a gun. As I looked at Arafat, I sensed we both had been forged of steel in the paths of our lives. I felt as if I knew him—his pain and hurts.

As we sat down, I said, "Sir, it's 2:00 A.M. You have had a long day and a long struggle. I'm not here as a politician, a diplomat, or a reporter. You've met plenty of those. I'm here as a simple man with a cross. And I would like to read you some of the words of Jesus."

I started reading from the Sermon on the Mount in Matthew 5: "Blessed are the poor in spirit. . . . Blessed are those who mourn. . . . Blessed are the meek. . . . Blessed are those who hunger and thirst for righteousness. . . . Blessed are the merciful. . . . Blessed are the pure in heart. . . . Blessed are the peacemakers."

I read and shared about many more Scriptures. Then I took his hand and said, "Let's pray." I knelt and talked to God for about fifteen minutes, crying as I prayed. Arafat had taken my hand with both of his hands, and tears filled his eyes. When I finished praying, he spoke softly: "There is no doubt the Bible is more powerful than the gun or the sword. The Romans tried to kill Christians. They beat, imprisoned, and murdered them. But slowly the believers, the Christians, took Rome, and Rome became Christian. They took it by the heart. They did with the cross what no army had done."

We talked for about two more hours. I explained how Jesus died for us and why he is the way, the truth, and the life. Finally, I asked Arafat to join me in praying a prayer of commitment to Christ. "Dear Lord Jesus, come into my heart. Cleanse me. Save me."

He squeezed my hand as I prayed, but he didn't repeat the words of the prayer. When I asked Arafat if he had accepted Jesus into his heart, he simply smiled and told me about a Christian friend of his.

As I prepared to leave, I gave him a small, simple cross. Arafat responded with a more extravagant gift: a two-foot long mother-of-pearl cross from the Holy Land.

"Sir," I said, "if you will lay down your weapons, I will pick up my cross and walk alongside you into Jerusalem."

Arafat didn't respond to my offer. But as his men drove me to my room about five o'clock that morning, I reflected on the fact that I had just been with one of the most gentle and kind men I had ever met. We didn't agree on everything, but we became friends. As I would see, that friendship continued for many years.

Called to Return

Two years later, in the summer of 1982, I carried the cross through Scandinavia with my son Joshua (age eleven) and my daughter Joy (age thirteen). On Sunday morning, June 27, I picked up a Swedish newspaper and saw a photo of Yasser Arafat on the front page. A cease-fire forged by the United Nations between Israel and the PLO had fallen apart. War had again broken out in the Middle East.

Immediately I felt the Lord calling me to return to this land. I said to God: *If you will have some other evangelist go, then I won't need to go to this war.* But as I looked through the newspaper, there was no evidence that Billy Graham or the pope or any other Christian leader was going to Lebanon.

Then something amazing happened. While Joy, Joshua, and I were praying, Joshua looked up and saw Jesus standing behind me as I prayed. Jesus spoke to Joshua and said, *Joshua, go with your father to the other countries as far as you can.* Joshua told me about his vision, and we knew we had to go.

But I wrestled a great deal with this call. How could I take my son into this horrible war? There was no choice. I had to go to Lebanon. Here I was in beautiful Scandinavia; we had just arrived in Sweden, and I wanted so much to continue to Stockholm with the cross. But war and death were raging in Lebanon and had to be offset with the good news and life. Joy flew back to Los Angeles, and Joshua and I booked the first flight to Israel.

I explained to Joshua as best I could about the war-torn region that was our destination. "You know," I said, "thousands of years ago a man of God named Abraham had two sons, Ishmael and Isaac. The descendants of Ishmael became the Arabs, and the descendants of Isaac became the Jews. These two groups have been fighting for thousands of years. Christians are involved, too, because Jesus was a Jew and came from this part of the world. Jews, Christians, and Muslims all claim to follow the same God, but in the last few decades, tensions between these groups have broken out into conflict and war. This latest battle started because the PLO and other groups were attacking Israel, so the Israeli army invaded Lebanon to drive out the PLO and stop the attacks."

I don't know how much my explanation helped, but as Joshua and I traveled to this troubled land, we sensed that God could use us to relieve the tensions a bit. Or at least that was our prayer.

Chaos

When we arrived at the airport in Tel Aviv, Israel, we had to figure out how to get to West Beirut. I felt the Lord wanted us to speak with Yasser Arafat and the people there again. But now the Israeli army, which was pounding the outgunned PLO and Syrian forces in the city, surrounded Beirut. Still, Joshua and I rented a small car, tied our crosses on top, and started driving toward West Beirut.

We encountered roadblock after roadblock. When we got to the Lebanese border, we were turned back. "Come back tomorrow," said the soldiers.

A young man from Youth With A Mission who was known to the Israeli army went with us to the border the next morning and helped us get permission to go a few miles into Lebanon to the Israeli army headquarters there. When we arrived, we asked for a travel pass.

"It is impossible," they told us.

Joshua and I prayed and drove into a small town. We entered a restaurant to get something to eat, and I began speaking to a young woman there who happened to be from Scandinavia.

"The Lord told us to come to West Beirut to talk to Arafat and the people there," I told her.

"Shhhhh!" she said. "Don't say that here. We are the ones they are fighting."

Then I explained our mission to her and how we needed to get permission to go on. She said, "My boyfriend is a bodyguard for one of the men you need to see—one of the commanders."

She introduced us to her boyfriend, who then took us to the commander's home. The commander was so kind and wonderful to us. He agreed to give us the pass we needed, but he begged me not to take Joshua into the battle zone.

"I'll go with Daddy," Joshua said.

"But the PLO will kill you!" replied the commander.

"No," I said, "I don't think they will kill us. In fact, they would probably say that *you* would kill us."

As we drove toward West Beirut, we were stopped at about thirty roadblocks, where Israeli soldiers wondered how we had gotten a pass.

"Jehovah is our friend, and he wants us to take the cross into Beirut," I would reply.

Into the Crossfire

It's one thing to discuss war. It's another thing to experience war at close range.

We could see Beirut just ahead of us. The roads were full of troops, tanks, and armored cars. The sky lit up with artillery and rocket fire. Guns roared and flashes of fire filled the air.

Joshua, never having experienced anything like this, began to cry. I held him in my arms as we stopped on the roadside. "Joshua," I said, "I will take you back and return here alone."

"No, Daddy," he said through his tears. "Jesus told me to go with you as far as I can. I can't turn back. I'll stay with you. Jesus is with us. Let's go; I'm okay."

He gave me a little smile and looked ahead. I gunned the accelerator and raced up the winding road without saying a word. But in my heart I could feel the glory of God. This was God's mission for us. We were under the orders of our Commander. Maybe we would die in carrying out our orders, but we would not flee.

We met some Christian monks who lived in the area. They let us sleep in their monastery, which was located high atop a mountain. These monks were also worried for us. "Please let us keep Joshua tomorrow when you go to Beirut," they pleaded. "You will die. They killed one of our monks today."

Joshua, lying beside me on the single cot, went to sleep in my arms. A candle was my only light. I could see from the mountaintop to the darkness below. Beirut was being pounded by land, sea, and air. Flashes of light lit the sky. As I was praying and thinking, a mosquito began to circle my arm.

I thought, *Well, tomorrow I may die. Why not let this mosquito get its fill?*

The mosquito landed on my arm, and I waited for it to enjoy its feast. But the moment it tried to bite me, it began to shake. Then it flipped over onto its back, kicking its legs a few times until it didn't move again. It was dead!

I sensed the Lord's wonderful protective presence and these words: *My glory is upon you. Tomorrow night you will sleep in West Beirut.*

As tears flooded my eyes, I hugged Joshua tighter to my chest and fell asleep.

Glimmers of Hope in the Midst of War

Joshua and I experienced so many amazing things during our time in Lebanon that we could write an entire book about them.

> There was the man in East Beirut who watched over our car for us day and night.

> There was the man who ran up to us, ripped off his shirt, tore it apart, and tied a strip of white cloth on the top of each of our crosses. He wept as he did so, and he said, "You will die if you go in there." He made the sign of the cross and walked on.

For Joshua and I to enter West Beirut, we had to walk through a minefield two blocks long in the middle of five armies fighting. As we crossed into West Beirut, the PLO militants welcomed us with pointed guns.

"What are you doing?" they asked.

"We are carrying the cross," I replied. "We have good news. God loves you! Jesus is alive!"

A few minutes later Yasser Arafat came out of a building and approached us. His eyes were sparkling, and he was smiling and happy. He hugged Joshua, and we looked at each other. It had been two years since we last met. We hugged and kissed each other; then I told him how we had struggled to get there and how God had called us.

"I expected you would come," he said. "You are welcome!"

As we talked, Arafat said he had been told that we walked through a minefield to see him. As at our first meeting, I gave him a cross—this time a small cross I made out of two pieces of wood taken from the cross I carried. He graciously received this gift and kept it with him until his death in 2004.

> There were Muslim shop owners who stopped us as we passed with our crosses and asked us to pray for the safety of their shops.

Many soldiers at numerous border crossings and roadblocks refused to let us pass until I persuaded them that we were on a mission from God. Then they would relent, let us pass, and bless us, saying, "God be with you."

> There was the Syrian soldier who saw us with our crosses and handed me the badge from his shirt.

Reporters and photographers from ABC, CBS, NBC, CNN, *Time*, *Newsweek*, Associated Press, and Reuters were so desperate for something positive amid the death and destruction that they mobbed Joshua and me. They delivered our message of hope to a global audience.

> There was one sentence people on both sides of the conflict said to us many times: "We welcome you, but the other side will kill you."

As Joshua and I walked together—father and son, each of us carrying a cross—I could see what a powerful impact we were having on people. They were touched by our willingness to walk among them as ambassadors of peace.

Beauty in Ashes

As Joshua and I walked with our crosses in Beirut, we heard the screams of the dying. We heard the cries of people trapped in bombed buildings. We saw diving planes and falling rockets and heard the shrieking sound of explosives as they tore apart everything they struck.

Walking in Beirut one day, Joshua and I came upon the scene of an apartment building shortly after it had been hit by a bomb. Human body parts were scattered throughout the rubble. We began to help those who were using sticks to collect the remains for burial. We wept as we picked up these pieces of men, women, and children whom God loved and for whom Jesus died.

Then I looked down the street and noticed that, in the ashes where a bomb had exploded sometime before, a flower was growing. When I saw that flower, I sat down and I cried and I smiled. That's one of the most inspiring things I've ever seen—out of ashes beauty can grow. And so it is with the hope of Christ. He died for us; he knows suffering. But he rose again. His resurrection life brings hope in a troubled and confused world, even in a world ravaged by hate and war.

Centuries ago, at a time when Christians and Muslims were killing each other during the Crusades, a man named Francis of Assisi crossed enemy lines to tell Muslim leaders about Jesus. Like Francis, I want to be one of Jesus' blessed peacemakers. What about you?

The Way of Peace in Northern Ireland

The conflict between Protestant Unionists (or Loyalists) and Catholic Nationalists (or Republicans) tore apart Northern Ireland for decades and killed thousands of citizens. British troops tried to keep things under control, but terrorist bombings and sniper fire were part of normal life for many people.

In 1972 evangelist Billy Graham wanted to visit Northern Ireland. I had met Billy the year before, and he asked me to accompany him in Northern Ireland, since I had been there previously. He wanted me to take him to the streets of Belfast so he could meet people face to face. His team wanted us to have the protection of armed guards, which was reasonable, but I refused. I promised no harm would come to him and informed the IRA of our plans.

I gave Billy a supply of little red peel-off Jesus stickers. He stuck one low on his chest, about stomach level.

"Oh no!" I said. "Don't put it there."

"Why not?" he asked.

"Because if you get shot at by a sniper, they'll use that red dot as a target. If you are hit, it'll take you all day to die. But if you put it here," I said, pointing to Billy's heart, "you'll go just like that"—and I snapped my fingers.

He grabbed the sticker and stuck it over his heart! It stayed there all day.

Soon Billy felt at home. As we walked, he handed Jesus stickers and gospel tracts to British soldiers in their bunkers and to other people, speaking to them about Christ. Then we heard someone calling to us from a bombed-out building on the Catholic side of the street: "Hey, preacher! Come over here and preach to us. It's Sunday morning and we're all inside."

I shared a simple gospel message with about forty-five people who were drinking and smoking in an illegal pub inside the bombed-out building. When I finished preaching, everyone applauded.

Later Billy and I knelt and prayed between the barbed wire and barricades at the "peace line" separating the Protestant and Catholic areas of Belfast. The evidence of violence around us broke our hearts, yet we prayed as God's servants in the midst of the conflict, seeking to change hearts and promote faith, hope, and love.

The funniest thing happened when Billy began sharing Jesus with a man on the Protestant side of the street.

"Well," said the man, "if I ever met Billy Graham, I think I'd get saved. He's the only one that gets to me. I'd like to meet him."

The man hadn't recognized Billy in his sunglasses and hat. So I spoke up. "Sir, today is your day of salvation. I want you to meet Billy Graham!"

Billy took off his hat and sunglasses. The man fell under deep conviction. It was so wonderful to see Billy kneel with the man, who prayed to accept Christ.

Thank God that, since the time Billy Graham and I walked the streets of Belfast, peace has come to Northern Ireland.

Chapter 8

Sharing Jesus with All Kinds of People

ISRAELI EGYPTIAN BORDER

Oh Father, you are amazing. My mind is swimming from the events of the last twenty-four hours. I couldn't even script a movie with what has happened today. Last night I slept in the home of Prime Minister Begin; tonight I'm lying in this little bed in El Arish. Yesterday's lunch was C rations from the Israeli army; today I ate at the presidential palace in the Sinai (although my arm still hurts from the guard dog that attacked me last night).

Today I prayed with the Egyptian commander of the Sinai to receive Jesus.

I pray for peace between Israel and Egypt. No more

war between these two in Jesus' name.

   Jesus, you crossed this desert as a child, and
it is incredibly harsh even today. I can hardly see
as the blowing sand gets in my contact lenses and
scratches my eyes. It truly is a walk of faith!
Oh Lord, how my back aches from the cross,
loaded and heavy with the backpack tied onto it.
But, God, you know this Sinai well, and I know you
will lead me through it.
I wonder what the next
twenty-four hours will hold
and where I'll be sleeping
tomorrow night. I'm glad
you don't have to sleep,
Lord. Good night anyway.

I have walked with the cross in every nation. As a result, I have shared Jesus with individuals from all the world's major religions, cultures, and racial groups.

Sometimes when I tell people that, they seem surprised. "Don't you run into problems?" they ask me.

"No," I respond, "the welcome for the cross has been wonderful from people all around the world. If this wasn't the case, I wouldn't be alive!"

Some people don't believe me, because they think of religion as something that creates conflict and tension. But while *religion* certainly may become a source of anger and animosity, *Jesus* doesn't need to stir people's anger. In fact, I find that people around the world *like* Jesus and want to know more about him.

I learned this lesson early on, during my ministry on the Sunset Strip in the 1960s. I talked to many hippies who were opposed to all kinds of things, including organized religion. But they didn't have anything against Jesus. They liked hearing about him.

I've seen the same thing in Muslim countries. Some people say there is a new global war between Muslims and Christians. But that's not what I see when I talk to Muslims. Jesus is mentioned more than twenty-five times in the Qur'an. Although Muslims don't easily commit their lives to Jesus, they love talking about him.

Today many people feel the same way Mahatma Gandhi felt. The famous Indian leader once said, "I like your Christ; I do not like your Christians. Your Christians are so unlike your Christ."

I try to counteract these negative attitudes when I walk with the cross. Instead of talking about Christianity, I try to focus on Christ and the love and grace of God. Instead of inviting people to church, I invite them to a banquet that Jesus is hosting. It's a wonderful banquet, complete with good food and good friends. The only thing you have to do to get in is accept the invitation Jesus has been sending for the past two thousand years.

In this chapter I want to focus on how followers of Jesus can talk to others about him without being caught up in arguments and dead ends. And as I have found in my life, sometimes you don't have to do anything special; you just need to show up and be available.

The Man Who Had Already Seen Jesus

Denise and I walked with the cross in Colombo, the capital of Sri Lanka. This island nation is predominately Buddhist, but it also has a large population of Muslims and Hindus as well as some Christians. A man dressed in a business suit began speaking to Denise excitedly.

"I've seen this!" he said, pointing to the cross and me. "I was sick and dying one night, but a man came to me and said I should follow him. Afterward I was immediately well. After that, I began praying only to this man, but I did not know his name. Passing a store one day I saw a picture of him. He was hanging on a big cross like this. I said, 'This is the gentleman who healed me!' I bought the picture and took it home."

The man had never even heard of Jesus. I told him my name was Arthur Blessitt, but the man on the cross was Jesus. We told him that we would get him a Bible, which would tell him more about Jesus. We helped the man understand who Jesus is and how to receive him as Savior and Lord. We prayed with him as he welcomed Jesus into his life. What a joy to share with this man to whom Jesus had already revealed himself!

And as we talked to other people in Sri Lanka we didn't talk about Christianity or Buddhism or Islam or Hinduism. We talked about Jesus.

Lifting Up Jesus

When I walk with the cross I don't promote myself or my personal opinions about theology or anything else. I focus on lifting up Jesus so all can see him.

This is a powerful thing to do, as Jesus himself said in John 12:32: "I, when I am lifted up from the earth, will draw all men to myself." Jesus was talking about his crucifixion (and probably his resurrection and ascension), but he is still drawing people to himself today. Jesus welcomes all people to come to him; and our job as followers of Jesus is to let people know about that welcome in ways that make sense to them.

As the following stories from around the world show, that welcome is attractive to Buddhists, Hindus, Muslims, and Jews everywhere.

Sharing Jesus with Buddhists

Some people say Japan is a difficult place to tell people about Jesus, but that was not our experience in the Okinawa Islands. In 2003, Denise and I—along with Junko, our interpreter; Pastor Dave Lukasiak, and about fifteen people from Dave's church—had a wonderful visit there.

I stood on the sidewalk with the cross on my shoulder in the main shopping district of Okinawa. The others handed out gospel materials (which were in Japanese) and Jesus stickers (which were in English). I began explaining to six young men who Jesus is and how he could be their Savior. As they were ready to pray to receive Jesus, I looked up to see groups of people lined up, waiting to come to the cross and hear about Jesus.

Most of these people were young. I needed to spend a lot of time with them because they knew so little about Jesus. After I prayed with a group, others on our team followed up, and I would begin with a new group. This went on and on!

I will never forget one man. I explained the good news of Jesus to him. After we prayed together, he asked, "Now is my name in that book in heaven?"

"Yes," I declared, and he was so happy.

Welcome to the new Japan!

Denise and I felt fortunate just to gain entrance to the Kingdom of Bhutan, located in the Himalaya Mountains, let alone to carry the cross there. The government heavily regulates tourism in order to preserve the country's traditional culture and the environment. In addition to that, Buddhism is the state religion, and proselytism is against the law.

We soon discovered that the guides escorting us had no idea who Jesus was or what the cross was about. Denise shared with them, starting at the beginning with Adam and Eve. She told the two young men, dressed in traditional knee-length, brightly colored robes, how Jesus died for their sins. Tashi, the interpreter, interrupted Denise and said, "This is horrible how Jesus had to suffer on the cross and die. I've never heard anything so sad." He was in tears.

Denise led both of them in prayer to receive the risen Christ. Soon their tears of sadness were replaced with joy.

Sharing Jesus with Hindus

The Indian subcontinent is the birthplace of Hinduism. Still, India has been one of the most welcoming places on earth. When I travel there with the cross, thousands of people line the highways to see the cross, to touch the cross and me, and to have me pray the blessings of Jesus upon them. The people of every community would garland my neck with flowers, welcoming Jesus and the cross.

Hindus believe in reincarnation, and this concept is very important to them. I used this concept as a bridge when talking to Hindu people on the Indonesian island of Bali about Jesus' crucifixion and resurrection.

"I understand that," one man said. "Jesus was reincarnated!"

"No," I replied, "Jesus came back in the same body." I explained how Jesus was resurrected, not reincarnated, and how he showed his disciples his hands and his feet that had been pierced.

Some of those we talked with began to understand the unique nature of Jesus and welcomed him into their lives.

Not all Hindus live in Asia. I talked to an elderly Hindu man in South Africa. He was excited to see the cross and invited me to come into his house. He took me to his bedroom, where a picture of Jesus hung on the wall. He explained that just a few days earlier he saw a vision. As the cross rose from the ground, he approached it. He placed a great garland of flowers on the cross. Then he heard a voice from behind the cross announce, "Soon the Big Father will come to you."

You can understand his excitement, since this day the cross did come to him! We prayed together, and he welcomed Jesus into his heart.

Sharing Jesus with Jews

I walked with the cross in Israel when a man stopped his car, got out, and said to his wife, "Meet a man who loves God, who loves peace, and who wants nothing."

We talked briefly, and the woman became curious about my logistics. "Where do you sleep at night?" she asked.

"Wherever someone invites me to stay," I answered.

"We would love to have you in our home," the man said. "But we are Jews. Does that matter?"

I laughed and replied, "Well, I was hoping to meet some of those around here!"

The couple stood the cross by the front door of their house and invited me in for an evening of food and conversation. They even invited their friends to come and talk with me. My hostess told me that she made jewelry but wondered why some people would want jewelry in the shape of a cross. I welcomed the opportunity to explain the significance of the cross.

Later I was walking up a mountain with the cross when an Israeli army bus approached me. So many of the soldiers wanted to talk to me that they invited me to come onto the bus, where I spoke to about eighty men and women. I shared about my walk with the cross and my love for Jesus. After I concluded with a prayer, the soldiers burst into applause and rushed off the bus—grabbing the cross, lifting it high, and taking pictures. I was crying, and so were some of the soldiers.

"Thank you for coming to us," they said. "And please stay on the road; it makes the world a better place."

February 26, 1980, was a historic date: Israel and Egypt exchanged ambassadors and opened the border between their countries. I felt the Lord wanted the cross to be one of the first things to pass through the border that day. I carried the cross from Jerusalem through Gaza, into the Sinai Desert, and on to the border, arriving February 25.

The Israeli troops greeted me with applause. I asked the border commander, Captain David Yaniv, if I could sleep there and be the first in line to cross the border the next day. Captain David smiled and said, "Anyone who has walked from Jerusalem will be first in line. Why don't you get a bed somewhere?"

"I have my sleeping bag. That will be okay," I answered.

He looked at the other soldiers, then said, "Just a moment." He returned in a few minutes. "I have a bed for you, if you like."

"Well, if you insist," I replied.

"Tonight you will sleep in the desert home of Prime Minister Menachem Begin."

"What?"

"Well, he isn't home. The troops are guarding it. The commander said it would be fine. Take your cross."

That night, with my cross in the living room, I slept in the prime minister's home in an Israeli settlement in an area soon to be returned to Egypt.

The next morning, all the Israeli soldiers at the border greeted me with warnings: "Those Egyptians will kill you with that cross. We've fought them for five wars in this desert. We like you and your cross. You are welcome in Israel—but Egypt? God have mercy on you!"

I told Captain David, "Jesus loves you, and you can know him."

He said, "I'm Jewish."

I responded, "Jesus was Jewish too, and he loves you and died on the cross for you. One day you're going to become a follower of Jesus."

Several years after our meeting at the border, David Yaniv received Jesus as his Savior as he watched *The 700 Club*. Twenty-five years later, we appeared together on a TBN program. "Captain David" is now the pastor of Roots Messianic Congregation in Lynnwood, Washington!

Sharing Jesus with Muslims

I did cross the border that day and carry the cross into Egypt. When I walked out of the immigration post, a black limousine was waiting to take me to El Arish. But I declined so that I could continue carrying the cross through the desert. When I arrived at the presidential palace in El Arish hours later, a red-carpet welcome was waiting for the cross and me. The military governor of the Sinai invited me into his office and asked why I refused his government's offer of an air-conditioned limousine in favor of walking across the desert.

"Because Jesus has called me to walk—to carry the cross around the world and to walk from Jerusalem to Cairo," I explained. "Sir, I'm a pilgrim on a mission from God. God loves you."

"But why the cross?" he asked.

"Because it is through the blood of Jesus shed on the cross that we can be clean. The cross is God's message of redemption and salvation."

We talked about Jesus for a while, and then we knelt to pray. I led the general in a prayer to invite Jesus into his heart to be his Lord and Savior.

When we stood up, he went to his desk and picked up a medal. "This is the greatest honor I can give you—the Sinai Peace Medal. Show this to anyone, and they will give you anything you need. Welcome to Egypt. Egypt is your land."

A few months later I walked in Jordan with my sons Joel (who was then fourteen) and Joshua (who was nine). It was the middle of summer, so we were hot and thirsty. We had also run out of food. Some soldiers saw us, stopped, and gave us water. Later we arrived at a Palestinian refugee village. The men there showed us wonderful Arab hospitality, kneeling down and washing our feet, dressing us in white robes, and seating us on a patio covered with grapevines. We were treated like kings!

When a man who could speak English arrived, they asked me what I would like to do. I replied that I would like to talk to them about Jesus. These Muslim men gathered around, and for hours I shared the good news of Jesus.

Inviting Everyone to God's Banquet

As Jesus explained in Matthew 22, the kingdom of heaven is like a king who prepared a wedding banquet for his son. The king's servants invited people to the banquet, but none came. They were too busy with other things. So the king told his servants to look harder for potential guests: "Go to the street corners and invite to the banquet anyone you find" (Matthew 22:9).

That's what I feel I have been called to do. And in a sense, we all have. God wants each of us to share with others the message of his Son. I share the following message with people at every opportunity.

The Message of the Cross

God created us and wants to communicate and fellowship with us. He speaks to us through the Bible and in our spirit and through the witness of others who know him. But since the sin of Adam and Eve, there has been a wall of separation between humanity and God.

God has worked to tear down this wall of separation, and often this has required the shedding of blood. "The law requires that nearly everything be cleansed with blood, and without the shedding of blood there is no forgiveness" (Hebrews 9:22).

Through Moses, the Lord instructed the people of Israel to put the blood of a lamb on the doorposts of their homes in Egypt. This protected them during the event known as the Passover. Then, on the Day of Atonement the blood of a lamb was sprinkled on the ark of the covenant in the Most Holy Place to celebrate the forgiveness of the sins of the people (Leviticus 16).

Still, the Old Testament prophets pointed to a future day when a perfect sacrifice would be made for human sin. That perfect sacrifice was realized in the person of Jesus, who was born without sin and who never sinned throughout his life.

Jesus taught the good news and performed many miracles, fulfilling the prophecies concerning the Messiah. He suffered and was crucified on the cross for our sins. God loved us so much that he gave us Jesus, "that whoever believes in him shall not perish but have eternal life" (John 3:16). As Jesus explained to his disciples during the Last Supper, "This is my blood of the covenant, which is poured out for many for the forgiveness of sins" (Matthew 26:28).

As soap loosens dirt and stains from a cloth so that water can wash it away, Jesus loosens us from sin and washes it away in his blood. It was only through his work on the cross that Jesus could forgive our sins. That is why the cross is so central to our faith.

Of course, the work of Jesus didn't end at the cross. Jesus rose from the dead, appearing again to his disciples and giving them the Great Commission to spread the message of the cross throughout the world. Then he ascended to heaven.

The message of the cross is for the entire world, so we should go and share it. I think we will be more effective in sharing Jesus' story when we do so in the following six ways.

How to Share Jesus in Our Complex World

As I carry the cross around the world and speak to people about Jesus, these steps help me reach more people more effectively.

Step 1: Follow Jesus

I am a firm believer in the sovereignty of God. It was God's will that the cross be carried in every nation; he brought it to pass and gave us favor, protection, and health to do it. I always say, "Jesus did it!"

What is Jesus calling you to do? Who is he calling you to reach? As you listen to him and follow his will, he will make a way for you to do it.

Step 2: Try Smiling

Some Christians look sad and depressed. But when I go out, trying to welcome people to the banquet of God, I am smiling and joyful. I don't go into the world to condemn people, but to give them a message of love and hope and salvation.

Step 3: Love God and Love People

When someone asked Jesus what the greatest commandment was, he replied: "'Love the Lord your God with all your heart and with all your soul and with all your mind.' This is the first and greatest commandment. And the second is like it: 'Love your neighbor as yourself.' All the Law and the Prophets hang on these two commandments" (Matthew 22:37–40).

When I walk with the cross, I eat with people and enjoy their food. I sleep in their homes. Their *casa* is my *casa*, and their family is my family. I love them as they are, and they usually do the same with me.

Step 4: Proclaim the Good News

For many people, "Christianity" has meant bad news. For example, many Muslims and Jewish people remember persecutions against them under the symbol of the cross. But when they see me with the cross and hear me share the good news, they understand a new and wonderful meaning for the cross. The cross is the sign of the love of God in sending Jesus. People the world over are very interested in this message.

Step 5: Don't Stereotype People

I see all the people in the world as a big family. Before I visit a country, I take what I learn about its history, culture, and customs with a grain of salt. That's because I don't want to carry the prejudice of history or the opinions of others with me. I want to encounter people one to one. As a result, I am free; and they can feel it. I love them, and they know it.

Step 6: Focus on Jesus

I don't use the word *Christian* to describe myself when I talk to people. Many people have preconceived opinions of Christians. Some remember that "Christians killed my dad" or that "Christians took our land."

When asked what I am, I say, "I am a follower of Jesus." Usually the reply is, "What is that?" That question gives me the opportunity to share Jesus.

And when I am asked, "Why the cross?" I share about Jesus' amazing role in our salvation.

Here's how Denise summarizes these six steps. When someone asks her how we are able to talk to so many people about Jesus, she says, "Arthur talks the same way to people, no matter what religion they belong to!"

And that is true. I never put down other people's religion. I just share with them about Jesus and let things happen from there.

Jesus and the cross are for all people of all religions. Everyone is welcome at the foot of the cross. My goal in life is to invite people to the cross. And if you focus on Jesus instead of all the issues that divide us, you can do the same.

Chapter 9

God's Miraculous Intervention

Believe me when I say that I am in the Father and the Father is in me; or at least believe on the evidence of the miracles themselves. I tell you the truth, anyone who has faith in me will do what I have been doing. He will do even greater things than these, because I am going to the Father. And I will do whatever you ask in my name, so that the Son may bring glory to the Father. You may ask me for anything in my name, and I will do it.
—John 14:11–14

FIRING SQUAD

I read in the Bible of miracles, and last night I experienced one. With the brightness of the light of God, the gunmen fell; and you, Lord, have let me live to carry the cross another day!

It's a day after God's intervention, a day after the pointing of guns and falling gunmen, and I'm still tingling with wonder and awe at your power. Now I must tell you, Lord, that I was prepared to die. You know that. I really felt those were my last moments.

When I looked up and saw the gunmen on the ground, then seeing them run off . . . I actually felt a deep disappointment. I've prepared for this moment; I've expected it. I was ready for heaven, but

you still have more miles for me to walk.

I am reminded of the Scripture "For me to live is Christ but to die is gain" (Philippians 1:21, my paraphrase). So I'll just go on until that time really comes for me. I know it may not be long because there is still so much fighting along this highway. It's true that life is only moment by moment. I live by the racing traffic and am but only one stumble from death. Somehow death makes me focus on life and meaning and what your purposes are, Lord. So lead me on, oh God; you hold my life and health in your hands.

I'll keep going until you call my name. Glory.

I realize that followers of Jesus today have various ideas and convictions on the subject of miracles, particularly the role of our faith in experiencing God's miraculous power. But while the sovereignty of God will always inject a strong dose of mystery into this topic, all believers can surely agree that God is a God of miracles and that God's Son, Jesus, brings glory to the Father through the manifestation of miracles. Furthermore, Jesus made it clear that his followers would continue his miraculous ministry after he ascended to heaven.

Sometimes we pray for a miracle, and things don't turn out the way we prayed. Don't lose heart. God loves you and is working in your life. No matter what happens, trust Jesus—and the Holy Spirit will give you the grace you need regardless of your circumstances. Miracles are happening that you just can't see right now.

God has chosen to work many astounding miracles in my life and in my journeys with the cross. They have been so incredible that there is no mistaking them. Miracles have accompanied us along the way in many places around the world. Wherever we go, we seem to experience the most amazing things. This chapter records a few of these stories. My goal in sharing them is not to focus on myself, but to inspire you to a greater sense of awe concerning God's majesty and power.

A Miracle in the Face of a Firing Squad

The following experience is one of those times when God chose to spare me in his own divine way. It was not because of my merit that I was given this miracle. Many others more holy than I have had the honor of being martyred for Christ. It was simply the sovereignty of God. He chose to extend my life for his purpose. As of this writing, my two companions in this experience are still alive. They too speak of this miracle in war-torn Nicaragua.

I carried the cross in 1978 on the Pan-American Highway south of Leone. At the end of a long day's walk I arrived where our four-wheel-drive vehicle, pulling a small camping trailer, was parked.

Mike Ooten was driving the truck, which was full of gospel

material, and Don Price, a veterinary doctor from Key Largo, Florida, was spending his two-week vacation interpreting and teaching me Spanish. They had driven ahead of me and were parked by the road, talking to some people who had gathered. A few homes, housing a small number of old people and children, were scattered nearby. The people said to Don and Mike, "Don't stay here. They will kill you. At night everything on this road dies. Go to the next town and sleep at the church. You will be safe there."

The civil war in Nicaragua was raging at the time. The popular Sandinista guerrilla movement was revolting against the Samoza dictatorship, and bloody terror was everywhere.

"I never run," I said. "We will sleep where we stop with the cross. I have learned you must face fear and overcome it, or it will haunt you."

An old man made the sign of the cross as we parked the truck and trailer under a tree. We opened some cold canned food, ate, and soon fell into bed. Mike was in the front bed, Don was at the back on the top bunk, and I was on the bottom bunk. I was so exhausted that I immediately fell sound asleep. The night was hot, and I was wet with sweat. Suddenly, a loud banging on the side of the trailer and the voice of a man shouting, "Narcotica policia!" awakened me.

I shook my head as I sat up in bed and pulled back the window curtain to look out. A gun was aimed at my face.

"Narcotica policia!"

I turned on the light, slipped into my pants, and opened the door. Guns were pointed at me. One short, middle-aged man put a pistol directly in my face, pushing me back and stepping inside. All of our assailants were dressed in either khakis or blue jeans and plain shirts. Most were in their late teens or early twenties. Several came into the trailer and looked around. Don didn't say a word, even though he spoke Spanish. Mike sat up in bed, wondering what was going on. He couldn't find his glasses.

"What's happening, Arthur? What's going on with all these guys?" he asked sleepily.

"Pray, Mike. Pray."

The short man waved his pistol toward the door. They took me by the shoulder and arm. As I moved toward the door, I snatched the truck keys. This was simply an impulse, for no particular reason. Maybe I thought they might want the truck—and they could have it if they really wanted it. Without doubt, these men were *not* narcotics police. The people later said these men were government troops; the government would say they were guerrillas. In either case, their mission was to rob, to kill, and to terrorize the land.

I began to speak in the little Spanish I knew, telling the gunmen that God loved them and that Jesus would forgive them and come to live in their hearts. No one seemed to hear my words. Since it was a clear night, I could see seven men with rifles and pistols, plus two others lying on the back of the truck with machine guns. *Maybe they wanted to rob us,* I thought. But then they shoved me next to the truck and ordered me not to move. They lined up about fifteen feet away, raised their guns, and pointed them toward me. Suddenly I realized they were going to shoot me. I was standing before a firing squad!

The cross was on top of the truck and difficult to get to. This is what flashed through my mind next: *If I'm going to die, I don't want to die without a Bible.*

All these guns were aimed at me as I quickly turned to the right, took two quick steps, and reached with my hand to put the key in the keyhole of the truck door. I was successful on the first try. I was thinking, *Even if they shoot me, I think I can get the door open before I die and grab a box of Bibles.*

The men shouted, "No! No!"

I swung the door open, pushed the front seat forward, and grabbed a box of Bibles. The gunmen had no way of knowing what I was doing. Only God knows why they didn't shoot. But I decided it didn't matter whether the front or the back of my body was shot—I had to get the Bibles.

I put the box on the ground and stooped down to get it open. The boxes of Bibles were bound with strong tape, making them almost impossible to open without a knife. I could see the feet of the men around me and feel their pull on my shoulders as they tried to get me up. Finally I got the box open. I thought I'd give them all a Bible, too, so I filled my arms as I stood up. But no one was there!

I didn't know what happened. All the gunmen were on the ground, flat on their backs! The short man who seemed to be the leader was lying inside the trailer with only his legs sticking out. As I walked toward them, they slowly got up in a daze. The short man sat at the door of the trailer, collecting himself.

"Do you want a Bible?" I asked in Spanish.

"We won't bother you," he replied.

I picked up a water bottle and offered them a drink. They all jumped up, ran to their truck, and raced off into the night without turning on the headlights.

I stood in silence. What had happened? It all took place so fast!

As I walked into the trailer, Don said, "We thought you were dead!"

"They were going to shoot me," I said. "But I opened the truck and got some Bibles. When I looked up, the men were on the ground."

"Arthur, we could hear the blows of meat against meat. We thought they were killing you. Then we heard them cry out, and then they fell backward. One of the men fell into the doorway."

The three of us sat there talking the rest of the night. At dawn, as I prepared to carry the cross down the highway, the people who lived nearby were waiting for me outside the trailer. They said, "We saw a bright light. God was there, and the gunmen fell to the ground."

That same night, in Phoenix, Arizona, Paul and Jan Crouch of TBN were in bed about to drift off to sleep. Suddenly Jan had a vision. The ceiling of the room lit up with my face. In the vision, she saw me about to die. Jan grabbed Paul and shouted, "Paul, pray! Arthur is about to die!"

Jan had been reading Billy Graham's book *Angels*. She prayed in her own special and beautiful way: "Lord, send twelve big angels down right now and deliver Arthur."

Soon they felt peace, and Jan said, "Arthur is okay now."

An Amazing Visit to South Africa

After walking with the cross across much of South Africa for almost four months late in 1985, I returned with my son Joshua in June

1986. I felt that Jesus led me to do a twenty-one-day fast, seven days each in the major cities of Johannesburg, Cape Town, and Durban. During those twenty-one days we stayed in central city parks. I wanted to be where all kinds of people could see and approach the cross and me. Except for taking a bath or using the restroom, I stayed outside twenty-four hours a day—sharing and praying with people and sleeping in a sleeping bag when I could find time.

South Africa was being torn by virtual civil war. The white minority was trying to maintain control over the black majority through the oppression of racial apartheid, and antiapartheid groups were striking back. The government had declared a state of emergency.

Shortly after we arrived in the city park in Johannesburg, a bomb exploded in a crowded restaurant not more than one hundred yards away from us. Soon there was a second explosion, this time in a garbage bin outside the nearby Holiday Inn. More blood, more broken bodies. Some victims were white; some were black.

No one knew if there would be more explosions. There was no place to flee to safety, but hundreds gathered around the cross that was now in the middle of their suffering. Their sincerity was indescribable as men and women stepped up and said, "I want to know Christ." As people prayed, weeping and seeking peace for their country, a bond of love and urgency formed around the cross—a recognition that the only one who could solve their problems was Jesus, because the root of the problem lay within the human heart.

Physical and Spiritual Miracles

The miracles of physical healing that happened in other countries were intensified in South Africa. A couple of hours after the bombings, a woman suddenly rushed to me in the park, weeping and smiling at the same time.

"What is this?" she asked. "What has happened?"

"What do you mean?" I asked her.

"I have been sick for years. I just went to the doctor today. I was walking along the pedestrian mall right there in great pain. Suddenly I was completely healed. I have no pain! I stopped, looked around, and saw that cross! What is happening?"

I explained our mission to the amazed woman and prayed with her to receive Christ. She went on her way rejoicing, saying, "I'm going to send my sick friends to this park!"

I had not even prayed for her; she had been healed by the sovereign work of God.

After witnessing this, another woman stepped out of the crowd. She was crippled with arthritis in her knees, elbows, and fingers. "Pray for me," she said.

When I prayed for the woman, God healed her instantly.

The first day of the first fast had begun!

Things like this went on hour after hour, day after day, for seven days in that park. The South African Broadcasting Corporation (SABC), the government television network, filmed many of these miracles and then continued filming in the other two cities I visited.

Another memorable incident involved a thirteen-year-old girl who had been crippled by polio in her right arm and hand. As we prayed together, the power of God healed her. Yet her arm was quite weak, since it had been immobile for over seven years. I encouraged the girl to exercise her muscles. She could raise her hand above her head, open and close her hand, and move her arm out. The girl was almost in a state of shock.

"How do you feel now?" I asked.

"Fine," she replied, "except for my thumb. It won't move."

I couldn't help but laugh. Her arm and hand were fine, and she could move her fingers, yet her thumb was frozen tight like her arm and hand had been. I took her hand in my hand. A small crowd gathered around. I prayed for her thumb, and suddenly she could move it perfectly. She kept wiggling her thumb. She seemed more excited about that thumb working than anything else. What a joyful time!

On another occasion a man about thirty-five years old made his way to me through the crowd and said he wanted to find Christ as his Savior, and he asked me to pray for his healing. The man was badly crippled in one arm. I explained to him how he could know Jesus, and he was gloriously converted.

Seven years earlier the man had been in a construction accident in which the bones throughout most of his body were broken. He explained how the doctors put bone and skin from his legs into his arm, resulting in horrible scars all along his right arm. His arm was frozen in the joints, with just a fraction of movement in his elbow and wrist. When I saw this man's condition, a complete healing in his arm seemed impossible. But I put my hands on his arm and prayed quietly.

There was a pop in his elbow and then a crunching sound as I touched his wrist. He could now straighten his arm and move his wrist. He reached with his arm to touch his ear, and then he scratched the back of his head. He was excited beyond words.

"I can scratch my head with my right hand," he said. "Oh God, what is happening?!"

The crowd, the man, and I were flabbergasted.

After this man was healed, an elderly woman who had suffered with an excruciating sore on her ankle for seven years approached me. Because of the pain, she walked on only the ball of her foot and was unable to extend her heel to the ground. She had seen many doctors over those years to no avail.

I knelt and prayed for this dear woman. As I prayed, her sore was healed, her pain went away, and her leg extended until her heel was even with the ground and she could walk normally. She began not only to walk but also to dance and leap—shouting, "Thank you, Jesus! Thank you, Jesus! I've spent all my money on doctors, and now I'm whole!"

You can imagine the response as word of these miracles spread around the city. In addition, an SABC TV crew filmed these last two miracles. Crowds, crowds, crowds swarmed the park as the miraculous power of God was manifest.

During these twenty-one days of fasting and prayer, we saw hundreds of people healed and thousands of people pray to receive Jesus as Savior. As huge crowds gathered, I shouted out for those wanting to accept Christ to gather in one group and those needing healing to gather in another group. We had teams sharing the gospel and following up with new converts, and we had other people praying for the sick. It was amazing!

Relational and Social Miracles

The other kind of miracle we saw in South Africa, along with physical and spiritual healings within individuals, was healing between people.

On the fifth day of my fast in Johannesburg, I witnessed one of the most wonderful scenes I've ever seen. People from all over the Greater Johannesburg area were praying around the cross, including many blacks who lived in the sprawling township of Soweto and were deeply committed to Christ. A group of white soldiers in uniform was also in the park. They had been called from the reserves during the state of emergency to patrol in nearby Soweto. I met these young men in a church earlier, so I knew they were likewise deeply committed to Christ.

Somehow the black residents of Soweto and the white soldiers met each other. They moved away from the crowd and sat on the grass. I saw them talking, smiling, and praying together. After about an hour I walked over and heard them sharing about their children and families.

They said to me, "Because of Christ and the cross, we are one family. Could we come over and gather around the cross and pray together for the healing of South Africa; for the end of hate, death, and injustice; for understanding, love, and peace?"

We gathered around the cross, and a throng of people joined us. We were smiling and weeping and praising God. I thought to myself, *This is the hope of South Africa.*

On Sunday afternoon during my fast in Durban, we held a worship service in a church that met in an old movie theater a few blocks from the park we were using. Thousands of people from all four of South Africa's racial categories—blacks, whites, Coloureds, and Indians—overflowed the premises. We sang choruses and worshiped the Lord as people tried to get into the building. Finally I stood on the stage, tears pouring from my eyes as I took in what was before me. And then I slowly said, "This is the new South Africa. This is the real South Africa. If only the world could see."

I read the account of the Lord's Supper in Matthew 26:26–29.

GOD'S MIRACULOUS INTERVENTION

Gathered together in remembrance of Jesus, we enjoyed a beautiful celebration of Communion. After we received the bread and the wine, I shared about Jesus washing his disciples' feet at the Last Supper, as recorded in John 13. I wanted us to follow Jesus' instructions to wash one another's feet, recognizing that believers are one family, one body—the body of Christ—not divided by race or language.

The only way we knew to foot wash with such a large crowd packed closely together was to give out prepackaged, wet hand wipes. I asked the people to wash the feet of the person on either side of them. That way everyone would wash the feet of at least two other individuals.

The scene that followed will live with me forever. There in South Africa, with a crowd that represented a mixture of all the racial groupings, people washed the feet of the person next to them and prayed for that person. They laughed, cried, smiled, and hugged each other.

These explosions of love, hope, and unity were a powerful response to the explosions of violence tearing South Africa apart. The nation's news media reported these outbreaks of spiritual unity that crossed racial barriers. South African TV made two specials of our time in the parks of those three cities. This period of miracle after miracle was a foretaste of the peace that eventually came to South Africa. Praise God!

Miracles of Protection

Many years before this, during my first trip to carry the cross in Africa in 1973, I lay in bed under a mosquito net, reading my Bible by lamplight. The wonderful missionaries in whose home I was staying that night had told me, "You can't walk across Africa, especially carrying a twelve-foot cross. You can't eat the local food; you can't drink the local water unless you boil it first. If you sleep in people's homes, you will encounter all kinds of bugs, diseases, and worms."

I prayed, *Jesus, I need an answer. They tell me I can't do this, but you have led me here.*

I know this may not be the best way to study the Bible, but I just opened the Bible and pointed my finger on the page that fell open. I began reading the tenth chapter of Luke's Gospel. Based on that passage, I committed myself to these four things:

1. Whatever house you enter, say, "Peace be to this house."
2. Stay in that house, eating and drinking whatever is set before you.
3. Don't move around from house to house.
4. Heal the sick who are there, and tell them, "The kingdom of God has come near to you."

I did walk across Africa, and on around the world—and this Scripture is how I lived. I have never been sick a day on the road from parasites or germs in the food or drink, and I have never had diarrhea or fever.

Every time I eat or drink, I pray: *Lord, kill them all. If there is anything in my body that should not be there, cleanse it. If there is anything I need and it is not there, put it in and make everything work perfectly. In Jesus' name.*

God has answered that prayer over and over, and I think that is a miracle. The protection I have received in many difficult situations is truly nothing short of a series of miracles.

You may never need to pray for the kind of protection I have needed, but you will need God's miracles as you walk along your own road of life. The miracles on your road will warm your heart and fill you with joy. I know it! This is the way of the cross, whether the cross is being carried around the world or reigning in your heart.

Chapter 10

Pilgrims
in the
Former USSR

HILL OF CROSSES

Oh Lord, you know I've seen a lot of the world,
but I have never
seen a place more
touching than this hill
of crosses. I look at
them and weep. They
are such a declaration

of people's
love for you.
What an
affirmation
of their
belief in God,
in the face of atheistic, oppressive communism. I
feel I can identify with their commitment, these
precious people, their fearless passion to be
identified with the cross. I am their companion in
the struggle to lift up the cross for Jesus.

It will forever remain in my mind the image of all those crosses reflecting the brilliant moonlight. I pray that I, too, may reflect the true meaning of the cross. Oh merciful Jesus, thank you for calling me to carry the cross into all the world. I am not worthy but I am blessed to be chosen for this mission to every nation. Today Denise and I walked among the thousands of crosses; as we continue may we truly live in the way of the cross. Oh, thank you, Jesus, for what you did on the cross. We glory in the cross. I love you, Jesus.

enise and I were sitting in a church meeting in Cape Coral, Florida, in the fall of 1991. As the preacher was speaking, I suddenly saw a vision of a map of what was then called the Union of Soviet Socialist Republics. In the vision I saw a line going through the nations. This line represented the roads we were to take as we drove and carried the cross. *The way is open*, Jesus told me—adding that we were to travel that coming winter. Later I bought a map of the USSR and marked the roads I had seen in my vision.

Pilgrims are people who travel for spiritual reasons rather than for recreation. A pilgrimage is a journey with a spiritual purpose. Life is a pilgrimage, in a sense, if you're seeking to live for God. And like life, every pilgrimage has a destination, whether it's the next place on a map or heaven.

Millions of people make pilgrimages every year. Christians and Jews go to Jerusalem to see the lands they read about in the Bible. A pilgrimage to Mecca is one of the five pillars of Islam. Hindus see the Ganges River as a sacred place and pilgrimage destination. But our pilgrimage to the former Soviet Union was different. It was a pilgrimage to carry the message of Jesus' love and salvation to an area of the world where faith had been greatly suppressed. For decades atheistic communism had gripped this region. Bibles had been banned. Preaching and evangelism had not been permitted in public. Spiritually speaking, the many people of this land experienced great darkness.

The former USSR was in turmoil. The member states formed independent countries, and only a couple of months before our arrival, the Soviet Union officially ceased. However, communist rulers remained in power in the member states, and there was great conflict, including demonstrations, to determine who would lead these newly independent nations. Russian troops were still stationed in most all the countries. In many places one group after another put up armed roadblocks in an attempt to control territory. There was fighting in a number of areas as portions of countries tried to break away. In the immediate aftermath of these incredible events, the economies of these nations and the standard of living of their people were in crisis.

As Denise and I prepared for our pilgrimage to the former USSR, we knew we would be forced to endure tough conditions. In addition, we knew that much of what we were about to do would be controversial, if not illegal. But we knew that everything would be okay, because Jesus had called us and he would be with us every step of the way.

From West to East

As we loaded onto the auto ferry leaving Helsinki, Finland, for Tallinn, the capital of the Baltic nation of Estonia, we watched the Western world vanish into the cold northern waters. It was March 1992, and we were traveling in the Land Rover, with the cross mounted on the side and some food and ten gas cans strapped to the top. We pulled a small trailer loaded with thousands of Bibles and gospel materials. We had a tourist visa for two weeks in Russia, but we had no permit for the Land Rover and no visa for any of the other countries we hoped to visit.

As we headed toward a turbulent, struggling land, nothing was certain except the presence of God. This was our prayer: "O Lord, thy will be done. Cover us with the holy blood of Jesus that defeats all the work of Satan. Thy will be done in us, on earth as it is in heaven!"

It was dark when we arrived in Tallinn and drove off the ship into the cold wind. We parked in a market area of the old city and raised the pop-up tent that sat on top of the Land Rover. The tent was made of thin cloth, so it was almost like sleeping outside. The wind howled as we climbed the ladder and settled into the tent for the night. We slept with our clothes on—including coats, hats, and face masks—even as sleet, rain, and then snow covered our flimsy tent.

At dawn we awakened to the cold, our water bottle frozen beside us. Snow was everywhere, and a strong wind was blowing. I removed the cross from the rack on the side of the Land Rover, prayed, and began walking. Denise and I got separated from each other in the city, but each of us returned to our starting point and began again.

The weather seemed to change constantly: first snow, then pouring rain, then a blizzard so strong you could see only a few yards ahead, then sun and cold, then snow again. The sidewalks and roadsides, packed with snow and ice, were slick.

During those first few nights it was so cold that the moisture from our breath and body heat froze. In the morning our bed was wet from the frozen moisture that had melted. As we continued our pilgrimage, wonderful folks sometimes invited us into their humble homes. But whether we slept in the tent or in warm rooms with dry beds, we rejoiced in our journey. No matter the conditions, Jesus was with us every minute.

We moved one step at a time, one day at a time, as we carried the cross toward our final destination of Moscow. You may never experience this kind of journey yourself, but I believe God has a pilgrimage he wants you to take in your life; and we pray he will use some of what we've been through to encourage and inspire you as you follow his leading.

The Hill of Crosses

After traveling through Estonia and Latvia, we arrived in Lithuania at a place called the Hill of Crosses. This hill, a popular pilgrimage site for people in the region, is covered with tens of thousands of crosses of every size and material. The Soviets tried repeatedly to remove the crosses, including bulldozing the site at least three times; yet this expression of people's faith in God rose again and again, overcoming the forces of atheism and suppression.

When we arrived just before dark, carrying the cross, an elderly woman who tended the grounds rushed up with a shovel for me to plant my cross among the others. I showed her photos to convey that I was carrying my cross around the world. She was so happy we had come.

That night we slept by the Hill of Crosses. As we opened the zipper of our tent and looked out, we saw the full moon just over the hill of standing crosses. We could only weep and marvel. How glorious that the cross, once a symbol of death and rejection, has become—through Jesus—the symbol of life, hope, and acceptance.

As we looked at the hill, we prayed: "Thank you, Lord, for calling us to be your pilgrim followers." So thankful to be where we were right then, we wouldn't have traded places with anyone in the world. Many famous people have been identified with many things. How thrilled we are for our lives to be identified with the cross.

Over the next few days as I walked and preached across this cold land, I encountered many thousands of warm-hearted people, in churches and along the roads. People flocked to see the cross. They drove from miles away and brought us more gifts than we could fit in the Land Rover.

As we approached Vilnius, the capital of Lithuania, we could see a huge crowd gathered around the Catholic cathedral in the center of the city. They were waiting for the cross. The news had been on television and in the newspapers, and this crowd of Jesus-loving people came to greet us and hear our words. Denise was given beautiful flowers.

A hush of silence settled over the crowd as I began to speak. Having no interpreter, I decided to pray first. I simply prayed face down on the stone courtyard. The crowd knelt in prayer as well. The only noise you could hear was my voice and the sound of the people weeping.

When I stood, they stood also. I began to speak. Because I was crying, I could speak only a few words slowly. A man in the back of the crowd tried to interpret my words. "We have come with the cross that you love—to stand with you, and to pray with you, and to proclaim that Jesus is alive and his presence is here," I said to the crowd. "Jesus loves you!"

Soon another voice joined in, interpreting the words with which the first man had difficulty. I concluded speaking and knelt. The people knelt also, and I led them in a prayer to repent, believe in Jesus, and commit their lives to follow him.

Then two men stepped to the front of the crowd. An elderly man with white hair and a white beard read from notes as a distinguished-looking man in his forties interpreted so Denise and I could understand. They welcomed us on behalf of those who fought against communism and led the revolt here a year ago that contributed to the crumbling of the USSR. The key leaders of the anti-Soviet independence movement were welcoming us! Later that day, the Catholic bishop greeted us and insisted that our cross be taken into the beautiful Chapel of Martyrs inside the cathedral, which is a sacred place dedicated to the memory of those who have been killed for Christ in Lithuania.

Our visit to Lithuania connected us with many pilgrims who loved Jesus and had served him at great personal cost. I will never forget the elderly woman who brought Denise and me fresh milk straight from the cow. She returned in the rain to bring us eggs and black bread. The next morning she arrived on her bicycle and, though she spoke no English, made it clear that she wanted to carry the cross. I handed her the cross to hold for a moment, anticipating that she would give it right back. Instead, she grabbed it and headed down the road—leaving behind her bicycle and me.

I watched as this short, stocky, weather-beaten woman, dressed in black, struggled to carry the cross mile after mile as the tears flowed down her face. Clearly, she was on her own pilgrimage. Finally, she stopped, gave me the cross, kissed me, and made the sign of the cross before getting on her bike and heading back to her humble home.

I loved that woman, and today her photo hangs in my office. What a joy to encounter her and the other fellow pilgrims we met during our journey.

Peace in the Midst of Conflict

As we crossed many more miles, we found ourselves in one of the region's war-torn areas. But not even war means that a pilgrimage must come to an end. In fact, we felt that God had prepared the way for us to pass through such situations.

One afternoon we were in Ukraine, approaching the border of Moldova. We saw troops near the border crossing. Denise drove ahead of me as I carried the cross; she would wait for me at the next roadblock. As I got closer to the roadblock, I could see that Denise had gotten out of the Land Rover and was talking to the soldiers. Around her were armed cars, troops in foxholes, and huge concrete blocks in the road.

The soldiers were very friendly. We talked and prayed together. They said we could take the cross past the roadblock. Denise drove around the concrete blocks and across the bridge into the disputed region of Transnistria before disappearing from my sight. I carried the cross into the war zone, as I've done many times in my life. Troops guarding the bridge on both sides did not move from their defensive positions. Soon I was "in." No one even asked for our travel documents.

Later we carried the cross through Tiraspol, the capital of the breakaway republic of Transnistria. We arrived at a big bridge the warring factions had been fighting over, and the troops all put Jesus stickers on their rifles. They wanted Bibles and gospel material, which Denise gladly supplied. She was going before me, so by the time I arrived, everybody looked like a walking Christian supply store!

As we moved through war zones, we found that God used whatever means necessary to keep our pilgrimage on the move.

After carrying the cross by the Black Sea, we headed toward Crimea. Everyone said there was no way to get there because the road to Crimea—a peninsula with just a small strip of land connecting it to the mainland—was closed because of the tensions between Ukraine and Russia. We arrived at a police roadblock. We were praying, since our entire cross-walk to the east was in jeopardy. I got out of the Land Rover with our map and asked for directions to Yalta. We acted totally unaware of any problem. I opened the map on the hood of the Land Rover. The guards were impressed with the color map and its detail.

As I talked with the men, God did it: he melted their hearts and turned the impossible into the possible! In order to get into Crimea, they showed me how to avoid the closed roads and take small roads not on the map. They didn't ask for travel papers but merely smiled as we continued on our journey.

Just as Jesus told us when he gave us the vision for this pilgrimage: *The way is open.*

God's Grace in Muslim Lands

Next we headed east into Asia to walk with the cross in Georgia, Armenia, and Azerbaijan. Crossing the Caspian Sea, we entered five Muslim areas that, now independent nations, had been part of the USSR: Turkmenistan, Uzbekistan, Tajikistan, Kyrgyzstan, and Kazakhstan.

One day driving in Azerbaijan, which is also populated almost totally by Muslims, we heard a strange knocking in the engine of the Land Rover. Before I could stop, smoke boiled up from under the hood, and the motor began to bang loudly. We pulled off the road where a couple of buildings stood in the vast stretch of desert. Oil covered the smoking engine. A huge cloud of black smoke came out the exhaust.

Disaster had struck! The engine had blown, and we were certain there were no Land Rover parts for thousands of miles. What would we do now?

A man came over, shaking his head, and looked at the motor. He spoke no English but indicated he was a mechanic and would try to fix the vehicle. We got it to his shop, a building with a ramp. He had only four wrenches and was amazed at the tools I had. While he and his helper took the motor apart, Denise and I prayed. They laid the parts on the sandy ground. A crowd of men soon gathered, and I was sure they would never find the parts to put the engine back together.

Several of the rods were badly bent. They used a hammer to straighten them. And then they put the engine back together, often looking for a place to put an extra part. When all was done, I turned on the ignition, and the Land Rover started like new!

The men didn't want money for helping me, but I put a hundred one-dollar bills in the mechanic's pocket. He couldn't believe his eyes. I had just given him about half-a-year's wages. We gave all of these Muslim men Bibles and gospel materials.

A mechanical breakdown of this magnitude could have stopped our progress for a week or even a month. But God in his grace prepared strangers to help us on our way. We were on the road again after only five hours.

Passing through Roadblocks and Barriers

When we reached the border between Turkmenistan and Uzbekistan, the head official asked to see our travel documents. He began demanding a visa for Uzbekistan. All the police were waving for us to turn around and go back.

Just when it seemed our pilgrimage would precede no farther in this direction, Denise rushed to the Land Rover and got our photo album of places we had been. When the official saw me in a photo with Yasser Arafat, he smiled, shook my hand, and waved us through the border! Within one mile we had to go through two more checkpoints with roadblocks, but Jesus got us through.

Every successful pilgrimage involves a series of roadblocks and barriers. But if Jesus has called you to follow him, he will make a way for you to progress. And just when things look difficult, Jesus brings a fresh breath of beauty and peace.

While walking with the cross toward Almaty, the largest city in Kazakhstan, I experienced one of the loveliest walks ever. The high mountains we crossed were in the distance. The land was open and filled with flowers in full bloom. For miles the fields were covered in red poppies. Denise and I stopped to run and roll in the poppies, enjoying the beauty of God. But soon things got even better. Before us stretched miles and miles of flowers: first purple, then blue, then pink, then all mixed together. These flowers seemed to be trying to outdo each other. What a place to walk with the cross!

The local people told us that this area was covered with flowers for only a week or so each year. We thanked God for sharing this brilliant display with us.

Return to Red Square

Denise and I carried the cross in Siberia, a part of Russian Asia, before reaching Red Square, the heart of Moscow. I had been there in 1988, carrying the cross during the days of communist domination. There were few signs of faith back then, but this time things were different. Many believers were in the streets singing and evangelizing. The cross didn't seem to have the dramatic impact it had four years earlier, but the people were still interested. We prayed with many to receive and follow Jesus.

I felt elated that for the second time we had the cross in the place that once was the world's seat of atheism. How futile is human effort to rise against the Creator of the universe.

We could see a cluster of perhaps a hundred or so people standing between the Kremlin wall and St. Basil's Cathedral in Red Square. Denise walked by with the cross, and soon reporters and TV cameras surrounded her. She did interviews that were broadcast throughout the former Soviet Union and in parts of Europe. This was the crowning event in our epic pilgrimage through the former USSR with the cross.

Pilgrims on a Journey

When this pilgrimage was over, we reviewed what we had done. We drove about twelve thousand miles, which is equal to nearly half the distance around the earth. I carried the cross about 650 miles in three and a half months. Along the way we passed through 230 armed roadblocks. Truly Jesus opened the way for us.

At every step of our journey, the Lord showed us which road to take, when to start walking, when to stop walking, when to drive, and where to park. He led us through wars and ethnic conflicts by giving us exact directions and his protective presence. Most of the time he even told us the best time to cross borders. Every time we needed gas, God provided a way to get it—and that was at times almost impossible.

Where Will You Go?

Where is God calling you to go? What is he calling you to do? And who is he calling you to reach? You may never go on a twelve-thousand-mile journey to foreign lands, but if you are a pilgrim follower of Jesus, you must listen to his voice and follow where he leads.

No matter who we are or where we go, followers of Jesus are pilgrims on a journey. We are following in the footsteps of Jesus; and as we walk, we share his love and joy and salvation throughout the world.

Chapter 11

A Pope, a President, and a Young Girl

MONTREAL

Earlier today I was wet, standing in this city with a wooden cross, crowds cheering for a hockey team. The cross seemed invisible. The church didn't want it, and the preacher felt uncomfortable. I felt lost in this city. But thank you, Jesus; you were with me!

You sent the African man to help my pain, the small woman to bless and strengthen me, and that teenage

girl to show me why I'm here.

So tonight as I walked back in the dark to get my van, I thanked you, Lord, and asked you to bless those disinterested people, the church, and the preacher. They broke my heart as I saw your cross rejected and ignored, but I pray it made me a bit more like you.

You suffered so much and gave yourself for our sins. Yet today so many missed seeing you and getting to know you. I know your heart must break with the pain. Help me to see the world through your eyes as lost and scattered sheep without a shepherd. You, Lord, are teaching me more about how to be a true pilgrim. May I be to others the blessing these last three people were to me. Show me how to be ignored.

Perfect my heart as I live every moment to the fullest. It was you they were ignoring and rejecting not me.

It's your cross, not mine.

But you did have the few, and they were enough. Keep my heart tender and full of love.

People often ask me, "What is the most beautiful thing you've ever seen as you've walked around the world with the cross?"

I respond, "People!"

One of the privileges of carrying a cross around the world is meeting all kinds of beautiful people. And just as Jesus related to all people, I have tried to do that myself as I carry his cross.

In our world today, it seems few of us desire or are able to relate to various kinds of people. Some people seem comfortable interacting with rich people but not with poor or homeless people. Some people like talking about sports with others who are into sports, but they're not as comfortable talking to musicians or artists or dancers.

My goal, as I serve as one of Jesus' ambassadors to the world, is to relate to all people, to communicate with all people, and to share the love of God with everyone I come across. That means showing love to a politician even if I disagree with his or her policies. That means sharing coffee and conversation with someone who might be considered a terrorist.

I want to tell you about a few of the most memorable encounters I have had with people over the years. Two of these situations involved world-famous people, while the other involved people you have never heard of. But in God's view, all are equally valued and equally loved.

An Audience with the Pope

In 1969 three wonderful single women, the Dorack sisters, read in a newspaper about the cross and me and began praying for me every day. Ten years later I was scheduled to preach at a Presbyterian church in Santa Monica, California, their hometown. They heard about me speaking and came to meet me. I loved these Catholic women at first sight.

The Dorack sisters then wrote a letter and sent one of my books to their good friend Father Maloney, saying, "Why don't you have Pope John Paul invite Arthur to come with the cross to celebrate ten years of his carrying the cross around the world?" I didn't know anything about this until I received a letter from Father Maloney, extending to me an invitation on behalf of Pope John Paul II to go to Rome, carrying the cross, and to meet with the pope on December 19, 1979. I called the Dorack sisters, and we praised the Lord together.

I carried the cross from the seaside into Rome and then to Vatican City. What a thrill to carry the cross past St. Peter's Basilica, considered the largest church in the world, and the Apostolic Palace, which contains the Sistine Chapel with its renowned ceiling frescoes painted by Michelangelo.

I left the cross at the rear of the Paul VI Audience Hall, where the pope speaks every Wednesday when he is in Rome, and was escorted to the front of the auditorium. About twenty people were there that day to meet and speak with the pope. Audience Hall was filled with people as John Paul came down the aisle, shaking hands and smiling. After speaking on the subject of marriage, he walked over and visited with about seventy-five children and adults with disabilities. His compassion was beautiful to see. Then he looked at me and walked across the aisle to where I stood. It was an awesome moment.

Two priests were on either side of John Paul, and they introduced me to him.

"Oh yes," said the pope, as he smiled and took my hand. "Bless you, and thank you for carrying the cross around the world. Thank you for bringing Christ to the people. God bless you."

I thanked him for his blessing and shared a bit of my mission of carrying the cross. Then I said, "Now here I am in Rome, the city of St. Peter and St. Paul, after all these years on the road. And I'm so happy to meet you. You have become a mighty voice testifying of Christ in our time. We must help everyone understand that it is not form or ritual, but a personal relationship with Jesus Christ, through repentance and faith, that saves a person."

"Yes, yes," replied John Paul. "It's in the heart that we believe."

Then I asked the pope a question. "Is there anything I can do for you?"

He seemed startled and looked deep into my eyes.

"What did you say?" he asked.

We were speaking in English, and I thought he didn't understand me, so I spoke more slowly. "Is there anything I can do for you?"

"No one ever asked me that. They always ask *me* for something."

Then he smiled and said, "Pray for me as you walk to Assisi, the city of St. Francis."

"Yes," I agreed. "I will pray for you as I walk to Assisi with the cross. And one day perhaps I'll go to Poland."

The pope grinned, since Poland was his birthplace. "Poland! Yes, maybe I'll see you there. I pray you shall go to Poland."

Then he pulled me toward him and embraced me. As his strong arms wrapped around me, I wrapped my arms around him. Tears filled my eyes as I prayed aloud, "Jesus, bless him. God, bless him and protect him."

"Thank you," he said, as he prepared to leave me and greet some of the others in Audience Hall. "God bless you, watch over you, and use you."

"Thank you," I replied.

As his escorts moved him along, I heard the pope say to me, "Bless you; bless your cross; bless your mission."

A Prayer of Salvation with a Future President

I carry a small journal with me wherever I go, and every evening I write down what happened that day.

Here's what I wrote in my journal on the evening of April 3, 1984:

> Midland, Texas
> A good and powerful day. Led Vice President Bush's son to Jesus today. George Bush Jr.! This is great—glory to God!

Today we know George W. Bush as the forty-third president of the United States.

I was in Midland preaching at an evangelistic meeting called Decision '84 at the Chaparral Center. The meetings were broadcast over a local radio station so people not able to attend the meetings could hear what we were saying. One of the people listening in was George W., who asked his longtime friend Jim Sale to set up a meeting with me to talk about Jesus. Jim is a dear friend of mine and was helping organize the meetings. The next morning the three of us met at the local Holiday Inn.

After shaking hands and exchanging small talk, George W. looked me in the eyes and got right to the point. "Arthur," he said, "I did not feel comfortable attending the meeting, but I want to talk with you about how to know Jesus Christ and how to follow him."

I was shocked. Few people I have met over the years are so clear about their spiritual need and so direct about addressing it.

I whispered a silent prayer: *O Jesus, put your words in my mouth and lead him to understand and be saved.*

Then I slowly leaned forward, lifted up the Bible in my hand, and began to speak. "What is your relationship with Jesus?" I asked.

"I'm not sure," George W. responded.

"Let me ask you this question: If you died this moment, do you have the assurance you would go to heaven?"

"No," he replied.

"Then let me explain to you how you can have that assurance and know for sure that you are saved."

"I'd like that," he said.

I then began to share some Bible verses that talk about sin, our need for forgiveness, and Jesus' death for us on the cross so we can know him and be saved. (You can read the verses on your own if you like: Romans 3:23; Matthew 5:8; Romans 6:23; Romans 5:8; Romans 10:13; John 14:6; John 1:43; Mark 8:34; Matthew 11:28; and John 14:27.)

"The call of Jesus is for us to repent and believe," I said. "The choice is like this: Would you rather live with Jesus in your life or live without him?"

"With him."

"Would you rather spend eternity with Jesus or without him?"

"With Jesus."

"Mr. Bush, I would like to pray a prayer for you and then lead you in a prayer of commitment and salvation. You can become a follower of Jesus now."

George W. listened closely the entire time, asking a few questions along the way. It seemed like he was ready, so I reached my hand to him and said, "I want to pray with you now."

"I'd like that," he said.

He held my hand in a firm but tender grip. Jim also joined hands with us as I prayed that George W. might know Christ and become a true follower of Jesus from that day forth. Then I asked him to repeat a prayer after me, praying with all his heart and considering each word to make it his own. His grip tightened as we prayed together.

"Dear God, I believe in you, and I need you in my life," I said.

He repeated after me. *Dear God, I believe in you, and I need you in my life.*

"Have mercy on me, a sinner."

Have mercy on me, a sinner.

"Lord Jesus, as best as I know how, I want to follow you. Cleanse me from my sins, and come into my life as my Savior and Lord."

Lord Jesus, as best as I know how, I want to follow you. Cleanse me from my sins, and come into my life as my Savior and Lord.

"I accept the Lord Jesus Christ as my Savior and desire to be a true believer in and follower of Jesus."

I accept the Lord Jesus Christ as my Savior and desire to be a true believer in and follower of Jesus.

"Thank you, God, for hearing my prayer. In Jesus' name I pray."

Thank you, God, for hearing my prayer. In Jesus' name I pray.

"There is rejoicing in heaven now!" I said. "You are saved!" Then I shared Jesus' words from Luke 15:7: "There [is] more joy in heaven over one sinner who repents than over ninety-nine just persons who need no repentance" (NKJV).

The three of us rejoiced together for a moment, and then I gave George W. some gospel literature and encouraged him to share with his wife and his friends what had happened. "You need to give your own testimony of what Jesus has done in your life," I said.

We talked some more, prayed together, and said farewell.

Over the next year or two George W. and I spoke on the phone a time or two. But I did not see him again until 1999 at a campaign fundraiser in Fort Myers, Florida. When I heard he was coming to the area where I was living, I felt led to go meet him again. I paid the required one thousand dollars for admission but felt it was worth the cost to see George W. again in person.

At the event I stood in a line of people who wanted to say hello to the presidential candidate. I was the third person to shake his hand.

"I am Arthur Blessitt," I said. "We met in Midland . . ."

George W. interrupted me. "Yes, you carried the cross," he said, pulling me toward him and giving me a big hug.

"Do you remember when we met and talked about Jesus, and we prayed together, and you invited Jesus into your life?"

"Oh yes," he replied, as others nearby listened to our conversation.

"I am very proud of you and your testimony for Christ," I said quietly. "I would like to have a brief prayer with you again."

"Sure," George W. said. "I would like that."

We held hands and prayed together like we had fifteen years before. Then he arranged for a photographer to take a photo of the two of us together. And after his speech he leaned over some other people to reach out to me. "Arthur," he said, "God bless you."

We shook hands and said goodbye.

I have prayed for George W. many times as he went on to become the president of the United States for eight years.

VIPs in God's Eyes

The pope and the president qualify as very important persons in the eyes of most folks. Three people I met in Montreal, Canada, in 1976 were anything but famous. Nevertheless, these persons were VIPs to God—and to me.

The Montreal Canadiens had just won the Stanley Cup, and this was the day the city welcomed home its beloved hockey team. Crowds lined the streets, cheering and waving. No one spoke to me as I eased my way with the cross through the masses of people. As I walked on St. Catherine Street through the center of Montreal, the weather grew cold, windy, and rainy.

I wanted to leave the cross in a safe location overnight, so I approached a large church across from the central city square. Looking inside, I saw a big wooden cross about the same size as the cross I was carrying. When I knocked on the door, a woman opened it. I explained what I was doing and asked if I could leave my cross at the church overnight. The woman turned to the minister to ask, but I could see him shake his head.

"I'm sorry," she said, "but we wouldn't be able to do that." She started to close the door.

"Please," I insisted. "It's just a cross. I'm not asking for money or anything, just a place to put the cross."

"We can't just keep everything people want to leave here," she said.

"But it's a cross!" I said, frustrated and shaking in the cold. I gazed at the tall church steeple, picked up the cross, and walked back into the celebrating crowds. Tears rolled down my cheeks as the cross was ignored and rejected.

While I stood waiting for a stoplight to change, a black man tapped me on the shoulder. Speaking with an African accent, he said he remembered seeing me carry the cross in Nairobi, Kenya. Being a follower of Jesus and recalling the big crowds gathered at the cross there, he said he was shocked to see everyone passing it by here in Montreal. The man was on his way to the airport, but he held me in his arms, and we prayed together. The love I felt from him encouraged my heart as I continued walking down St. Catherine Street.

After a while I saw a small woman, likely a little person, coming straight toward me. She was wearing an old dress and a torn coat.

"Mister," she said, "God sent me to lay hands on you and pray for you."

"What do you mean?" I asked, bending toward her.

"I was in my house, and God gave me a vision. He showed me a man carrying a cross on a sidewalk. Then he told me to come down to St. Catherine Street and lay hands on this man and bless him. Would you please kneel so I can put my hands on your head?"

Her love was overwhelming. "Ma'am, you sure can lay hands on me," I said as I got on my knees.

She laid her little hands—hands that were rough and calloused from hard work—on my head and prayed with great power.

"There now," she said, "I've done my job. You keep walking with that cross."

I stood and looked at her gentle face, which was old in years yet radiant with the love that knows no time. Then I spoke to her. "Well," I said, "God has told you to come and lay hands on me. Now I feel God telling me to give you all the money in my pocket. God told me to give you *everything*, so here it is."

She began to weep and told me how much she needed the money for food. We both were crying and praying as she walked away and disappeared into the crowd.

Once again I went on my way. As I entered a residential area next to a park, a lovely young girl who looked to be about sixteen years old came rushing up to me. She had long blond hair and deep blue eyes with which she looked straight into my eyes.

"You're the most beautiful man I've ever seen in my life," she said. "There is a glow around your whole face." Then she handed me a flower.

I was too amazed to say anything. I put the cross down and leaned against it.

Then she spoke again. "I'm an atheist. What are you doing with that cross?"

I told her my story of carrying the cross and how the people at the church had turned me away from leaving it there overnight.

"Where are you going now?" she asked.

"I need to find a safe place to leave the cross. Then I will go sleep in my van."

"Oh," she said, "you can leave the cross at our house just around the corner from here."

I left the cross in the living room of the girl's house and walked to my van.

The next morning I drove back to the house to get the cross. The girl gave me breakfast. As I was about to leave, I asked if I could pray for her.

"I know you don't believe," I said. "But I do. So let me pray for you. If there is no God, it won't hurt."

"Oh yes," she said. "Last night it felt so good to have the cross in the house. I put a blanket under the cross and slept there. Please do pray for me."

As we prayed together, she opened her heart to Jesus.

In less than twenty-four hours in Montreal, I had been ignored by uninterested crowds on the streets, rejected by people at a church, comforted by a black man from Kenya, blessed by a little person, and welcomed by a young girl who went from atheist to believer! And as I said, while none of these individuals were celebrities, they are loved by God and are on his list—and mine—of very important persons.

All People Are God's People

When Peter spoke to Cornelius and his relatives and close friends, it was the first time the gospel was presented to Gentiles. Peter knew this was a big event, since he said: "I now realize how true it is that God does not show favoritism but accepts men from every nation who fear him and do what is right" (Acts 10:34–35).

If God doesn't show favoritism, neither should we!

The Lord loves *all* people. And as difficult as it is to follow this divine example, that is what God wants us to do.

By reaching out to the rich and the poor, the powerful and the weak, popes and presidents, little people and teenagers, we show God's love for all people.

Chapter 12

The True Story behind "Blessitt for President"

BLESSITT FOR PRESIDENT

Lord, what are you doing to me? I am constantly being ignored or ridiculed or criticized or rejected. Yet you will not let me leave this presidential campaign. You make me go on just to be humiliated. You don't want me to win, but you want me to try. You have a mission for me, and I am committed to do it.

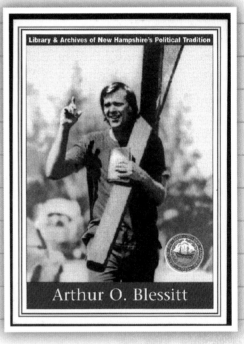

Library & Archives of New Hampshire's Political Tradition

Arthur O. Blessitt

Much of the water dripping from my face in humid Florida is not sweat but tears. Yet I wipe the tears and smile and press forward to share your love and salvation with everyone. It's hard to ask for a vote; I'd rather ask them to give their lives to you, Jesus.

Running for president feels uncomfortable to me. I sometimes have a flash of horror when I think,

What if I won?! Ha!

I ask myself, Which was easier—walking across Africa where I've just come from or running for president? Oh Lord, you know, the latter is tougher.

Jesus, you are stripping me of everything, and it is painful, but it is right. I want to be free for you to grind me to powder so you can blow me where

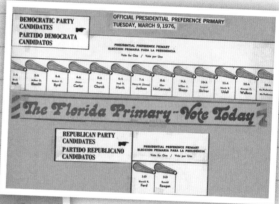

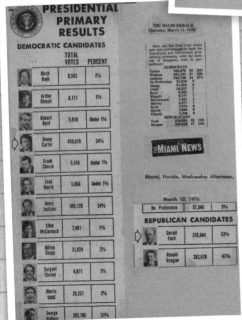

you will. Sometimes I think this campaign is more about me than anything else. You are at work perfecting me. Please don't stop now. I am a work in progress.

During nearly forty years of carrying the cross around the world, I've found myself in some difficult situations. As I conveyed in previous chapters, I have slogged my way through dense jungles and survived in the middle of war zones. But nothing was more challenging than running for president of the United States, which I did for seventeen months from 1974 to 1976.

Running for president wasn't something I thought up on my own. I didn't say, "Boy, I wonder if this would be a fun thing to do!" I wasn't yearning for power. I wasn't looking for a new line of work.

I had been carrying the cross for almost two years in Africa when the Lord called me to run for president. He even explained his reason when he gave me this assignment. I felt that Christ's plan was for me to run for president so that the other candidates would be challenged to tell the voters about their relationship with God.

At that time in America, religion and politics were two things most people didn't openly discuss. I know that candidates today talk freely about religion. Some wrap themselves in the Bible as much as they wrap themselves in the flag. But that wasn't always the case. Before the 1976 election, candidates didn't talk publicly about their religion. There were exceptions, of course. John F. Kennedy talked about his faith in 1960, but that's because he *had* to. He needed to defend himself against critics who said that, as a Catholic, he would be working for the pope, not for the American people.

Before the 1976 election there wasn't a movement of Christians called the "religious right," and even people like Jimmy Carter, who is known today as an outspoken Christian, didn't talk about being "born again."

But all that was about to change.

A Reluctant Candidate

Believe me, it would have been fine with me if Jesus had called someone else to get candidates talking about God. But he didn't. While walking with the cross in Africa, I scoured newspapers and listened to broadcasts of the BBC and the Voice of America to see if anyone else was raising the faith issue. They weren't, so I accepted Jesus' call.

I returned to America to enter the important presidential primaries in New Hampshire and Florida. I walked with the cross in both states from October 8, 1974, to March 9, 1976, the date of the Florida primary.

In leaving Africa for the American campaign trail, I was entering a war zone. My campaign would be a humiliating struggle unlike anything I had experienced before.

I would never have done this if Christ hadn't called me. But I did it out of obedience, knowing he had a purpose in it all that was beyond me and my petty concerns. If I had known the future, I would have trembled; but since I only knew the Lord, I was thrilled. Plus, I love a challenge. I enjoy something that requires everything and lifts me to new levels of discipline and endurance.

"As iron sharpens iron, so one man sharpens another," wrote Solomon in Proverbs 27:17. As I ran for president, I would be sharpened and strengthened in new and challenging ways that would teach me valuable lessons about reaching the world for Jesus.

The God Question

Most candidates have a slogan or campaign statement that is the focus of everything they do. For me the focal point was the God question. My goal was to ask the other candidates a question that had been largely avoided in presidential campaigns for almost two hundred years: "What is your personal relationship with God?"

I'm not talking about clichés, such as the words "God bless you" or "God bless America" many political figures use at the end of their talks. Some politicians speak these sincerely. For others, it is the worst form of pandering. I wanted to separate the sheep from the goats by asking each candidate what he thought and challenging him to go public with his beliefs.

My mission faced difficult challenges as I tried to work with a political establishment that didn't know what to do with me. Plus, I was handicapped by the fact that Jesus told me I couldn't accept a penny in campaign contributions from any person or organization. I ran as a Democrat in both New Hampshire and Florida, appearing on the ballot in both states. But I was denied the opportunity to participate in the debates, since only candidates whom the national news media considered the major contenders could take part in them.

I also didn't receive as much media attention as the other candidates, and the media coverage I did receive was mixed. Some reporters said I was nuts (and what I was doing probably looked nutty to them), but others were positive.

William Willoughby of the *Washington Star* said, "Give 'em hell (oops, I mean keep on giving 'em what you've been giving 'em), Arthur."

The *Nashua Telegraph* in New Hampshire ran a story with this headline: "Candidate Blessitt Emphasizes Contact with People." The article said that five hundred people were working on my campaign around the state.

Here's what the *Florida Times-Union* in Jacksonville, Florida, said: "What's a minister doing entering the presidential race? Because the millions of Americans who worship God on Sundays are being ignored, says the Rev. Arthur Blessitt."

I loved talking to the journalists. But the highlight of the campaign for me was the wonderful, beautiful people I was privileged to meet along the way.

A Grassroots Campaign

I carried the cross during my campaign in both states, and the reception of the people was powerful. They loved me, fed me, and helped me. I spoke in shopping centers and nursing homes. I also spoke on college campuses; I loved speaking to young people, who typically gave me standing ovations.

But most of the time I campaigned through something I called "house meetings." A family would invite me to speak and invite their friends and neighbors to attend. Typically I spoke for ten minutes about why I was running for president, and then I spoke for ten minutes about Jesus, followed by twenty minutes of questions and answers. I closed the meetings by sharing how the people could welcome Jesus into their lives, concluding with a brief prayer of salvation they could pray with me. Many times more than half the people in each house meeting prayed to receive Jesus as their Savior. Over the course of my campaign, thousands of individuals came to Christ.

The love and fellowship in these meetings were beautiful. The hosts and the folks who attended were nothing but friendly and appreciative. I left each house with people hugging one another, crying, praying, and praising God. I feel certain that I was more successful in evangelizing than I was in lining up votes, even though I received 1 percent of the primary vote in Florida and 1 percent in New Hampshire.

My experience with these house meetings made me think of the beginnings of the Christian movement two thousand years ago when believers met in homes. What would happen in our communities today if more Christians practiced hospitality by opening their doors to friends and neighbors so they could share Jesus' love with them?

Struggles on the Campaign Trail

Not everyone was so warm and friendly. Every effort was made to get me to withdraw from the race. Twice people shot at me as I carried the cross. Another time a man waved a gun in my face.

The Lord would not even allow me to have a driver for my van. I slept in the van at night and then carried the cross fifteen or twenty miles the next day. Then I looked for a house or business where I could leave the cross overnight. If I was unsuccessful, I hid the cross in bushes beside the road. Then I hitchhiked to my van, fifteen or twenty miles back up the road.

Sometimes I had to stand by the road for an hour or two before someone gave me a ride. My appearance began looking very unpresidential when I had to stand in the pouring rain.

"Where are you going?" people asked me when they stopped.

"Oh, about twenty miles up the road."

"Whatever are you doing out here in this bad weather?"

I didn't want to tell them I was running for president. I would pray: *Lord, let me witness to them about you. I don't mind sharing about the cross, but if I tell them I'm running for president, they'll think I'm crazy!*

Why do you humiliate me? You know what they'll think. No one will vote for a wet, poor, cross-carrying hitchhiker anyway. Why do you make me do this? You won't let me take money or even get a driver for my van. I can't win this way.

But Jesus was not swayed by my logic. *Tell them what you're doing,* he would say. So I did.

"Well, I've been carrying a twelve-foot cross around the world since 1969. I was in Africa when God called me to come back to America and run for president."

"Run for president? President of what?"

"President of the United States. I'm on the ballot!"

Each time this happened, I felt God was humbling me so he could exalt himself and make me into a better man. But at times I felt God had another purpose, too. Perhaps he was using me to change the course of history.

Challenging Jimmy Carter

Twice during the campaign I spoke with Jimmy Carter, the former governor of Georgia who eventually won both the Democratic Party nomination and the general election. One day when we were eating in the same restaurant in New Hampshire, I walked over to his table and said hello.

"Hello, Arthur," he said, greeting me by name.

After a few moments of exchanging pleasantries, I came right to the point. "Mr. Carter, you know why I am running for president. I'm raising the issue of each candidate's relationship with God. What is your relationship with God? Do you know Jesus as your Savior?"

He smiled and looked nervously at the reporters who were nearby. "You know I'm a Baptist, and you know what that means," he said.

"Yes, I think I do. But why don't you just say that you are 'saved' or 'born again'? I feel sure you really are. Why not just say so?"

Carter looked away. It seemed as if he was getting annoyed. I pressed on. "You can change history by sharing about your relationship with Jesus. There are huge numbers of voters in America who are very interested in this question. I'm going after them. You know about the attention I am getting. Most people won't vote for me because they know I can't win. But they would vote for you if you were up-front about your faith in Jesus. I'm going to pray that you speak out about your relationship with God. Just know that I will stay in the running until someone responds to this issue. God bless you, and may he give you the courage to break down this wall."

I wish I could tell you that after this meeting candidate Carter started speaking about his faith. That didn't happen. However, shortly after the Florida primary, he did speak openly about being "born again." Carter never talked to me about why he did this, but I believe he saw the impact of my campaign and concluded that people cared about his faith.

Character was an important factor in the 1976 presidential election. President Richard Nixon had resigned in 1974, following the Watergate scandal, with Vice President Gerald Ford completing the rest of Nixon's term. Americans wanted a president who had solid character and strong moral values. Carter's frank and open discussion of his faith helped convince many voters he was the man for the job. It also confirmed to me that my mission to help interject the question of the presidential candidates' relationship with God was accomplished. I left the United States to carry the cross in Canada and then on to the far side of the world. I was in Australia during the general election in November.

A Complex Legacy

Here's what is said about me in the archives section of the New Hampshire Political Library website (http://www.politicallibrary.org/cards/SeriesOne/blessitt.html): "This evangelist street preacher was a precursor of the 'Christian Right.' He was not politically motivated; rather he promoted religion all over the world. He campaigned in New Hampshire by dragging a huge wooden cross on a large wheel wherever he traveled."

I'm not sure I like being called a precursor of the Christian Right, but I do think I had an impact on the 1976 election—and perhaps political candidates have addressed issues of faith ever since. And sometimes that thought worries me.

My fundamental reason for running for president was to demonstrate that voters want to know what candidates for public office believe in their hearts about God. Are they followers of Jesus? Do they try to apply the values of their faith to the decisions—large and small—that they make every day?

If I had any role in making politicians more up-front about their faith, I am pleased. But I have been less pleased by the efforts of some believers to attach the "Christian" label to a long list of issues that seem to have little to do with Jesus: Does Jesus favor capital punishment? Does Jesus want America to declare war on another country? Does Jesus like Republicans more than Democrats?

It's good for followers of Jesus to have convictions and opinions about these issues and to discuss their views with passion and energy. But I'm troubled by the tendency of some believers to wrap Jesus around all their pet political issues. Transforming Jesus from a Savior to a politician is harmful; it diverts people's attention from the real Jesus, who loves and cares for them.

In his day, Jesus was called a friend of sinners. Men and women of all kinds could go to him and find love, friendship, forgiveness, and a new life. Sinners kissed him. They washed his feet. He ate and drank with them. Through it all Jesus was known for his love and tenderness and compassion for people with hurts and needs. His call to the hurting and sinful was simple and loving: "Come unto me and I will give you rest" (Matthew 11:29, author's words). But in the years since the 1976 election, some believers have increasingly attached Jesus to a series of divisive political issues. I'm convinced that this has done great harm to the witness of Jesus and has hindered many individuals from coming to Jesus for the love and forgiveness they need.

Sinners who need and want Jesus are sometimes pushed away by being made to feel they are despised or rejected by Christians simply because of differences in political party or policy. Jesus' ministry was one of love and mercy. Today some Christians condemn people who hold the "anti-Christian" position on a long list of political issues. In my experience, it is hard to mix mercy with condemnation. The world doesn't need a pointed finger of condemnation, but rather an outreached hand of love.

Do you remember the song that says, "They will know we are Christians by our love"? That's how non-Christian people should know us—not by our legislative agenda. Our public pronouncements should be like those of Paul, who said: "For I resolved to know nothing while I was with you except Jesus Christ and him crucified" (1 Corinthians 2:2).

I am thankful that our democracy allows Christians to be citizens who participate in the political process. However, I believe we must be careful not to allow our spiritual and moral convictions to be exploited and politicized by vote-hungry politicians. And we should not embrace our political views so tightly that they prevent us from embracing the men and women Jesus wants to love through us.

Chapter 13

Roads of Glory

*Now the Lord is the Spirit, and where the Spirit of the Lord is, there
is freedom. And we, who with unveiled faces all reflect the Lord's
glory, are being transformed into his likeness with ever-increasing
glory, which comes from the Lord, who is the Spirit.*
—2 Corinthians 3:17–18

GERMANY

after the Wall came down

Six hundred thousand footsteps marching on
the snow-covered square; 300,000 voices cheering
the uplifted cross! After almost fifty years of
atheistic oppression under the boot of communism,
the cross was welcomed in East Germany. For
as long as I live, I will remember the cheers and
welcome of the
cross. I'll never
forget the sea
of people passing
it hand over hand

toward the
front of
the crowd
or the
pushing and

shoving of those men and women in the freezing night trying to get to the cross to touch it or carry it. It's late tonight, and again Joshua is sleeping, and I'm recounting the historic and glorious events of today and visiting with Jesus, my road companion and Savior.

Oh Lord, I feel at home tonight; I feel one with them. We could not communicate, but in our eyes and countenance we knew each other's passion, commitment, and our common bond—the belief that some things are more important than life. Thank you, God, for letting me be a part of this struggle. They had risen up in peaceful defiance, ready to die, and we had come to join them. Oh Jesus, I feel such emotion and joy in my body. I have a taste of how heaven must be! Oh, I weep with joy thinking of this awesome welcome for your cross as I recall how often it has been rejected or ignored. But tonight, here, the crowds cheered it and meant it.

Should I never live another day I have lived! I have seen, felt, and touched the impossible come to pass. That wall I prayed to come down eight years ago is now crumbling! Glory I'm glad I lived to see this day! Oh, I adore you, my Jesus, and at least for one day in one place you were welcomed.

In the Presence of His Glory

In 1979 my daughter Gina, my friend Mike Ooten, and I were in Iquitos, Peru, which is nestled along the Amazon River. The awesome adventure of taking the cross by boat down the Amazon lay ahead. After an evening swim and back in my room, I began to read 1 Samuel. I study a part of the Bible on every trip. Just as I want others to be blessed, I too hunger and thirst for all the fullness of God and his Word.

The words in 1 Samuel 2:35 seemed to leap inside of me: "And I will raise me up a faithful priest, that shall do according to that which is in mine heart and in my mind: and I will build him a sure house; and he shall walk before mine anointed forever" (KJV). Flashing through my mind was the fellowship God had with Adam and Eve in the garden of Eden. God walked with them, spoke to them, and listened to them as they enjoyed paradise together. I thought of the horror of sin that came—but oh, how God must still want to fellowship with us.

Lying in bed, I prayed: *Lord, if there is anything you'd like to say tonight, you can speak whatever is in your heart and in your mind, and I will do it for your glory.*

Words cannot express the passion in my heart for God to reveal his thoughts. It was two o'clock in the morning when I went to sleep.

At three o'clock I was suddenly awakened. It was as if I could see far beyond the room into outer space. A distant fiery glow grew closer and larger as it swirled toward me. I tried to cry out, but I couldn't speak. Neither could I move. The mighty wind of the golden glory of God was rushing in, and I was being swept away.

A host of people and angels was just beyond the golden swirl of glory. The brightness just behind the glory was blinding—silver and ultra white—then these words appeared before my eyes: "Arthur, proclaim that the glory of the coming of the Lord is at hand."

Those words stayed before my eyes during the rest of the vision. From the bottom of my feet to the top of my head, like ocean waves, the glory swept over me. All strength left my body, and I lay as dead for four hours. I cannot tell all that I saw, but I experienced the glory of the coming of the Lord. How indescribably wonderful!

God's Glory on the Walk with the Cross

If you asked me to close my eyes and say what comes to my mind when I think about walking with the cross around the world, it would be the faces of those who gather around the cross. The faces are of many colors, and the people speak hundreds of languages. They may be smiling or they may be weeping, but they know that they are feeling the presence of the Lord.

I am not saying that I am holy or that the wood of the cross itself is holy; but I am saying the hand of God is upon this walk, and people experience his glory as the word spreads that the cross is coming down the road. Time and again I have seen people come in anger but melt into tears as they draw near to me and the cross. Hundreds of thousands of people have touched the cross or me and rubbed themselves as if they are blessed just by the touch. They feel something they have never felt before. I stop with every group and proclaim that it is Jesus who blesses and saves, and I share how to invite him into their lives.

The glory of the Lord touches people, because the Holy Spirit of God is present in such a way that they are drawn to the cross and Jesus. Even individuals who are devoted to other religions experience the miracle of God's glory that travels on the road with the cross and me. They feel love and mercy in a way they have never felt before. Only God knows people's hearts, but millions have heard the message of Jesus and prayed to receive him.

I often speak of the bubble of glory that seems to surround the cross, me, and anyone with me on a trip. Many say they have seen a glow surrounding the cross. But for sure I know that when people get within fifty to one hundred feet of the cross they are aware of the glory of God. They may not describe it in those terms, but they feel something within. Many get goose bumps or cry or break into a smile. I have seen people who were coming to attack me, raging in anger, become totally calm as they draw near the cross.

Hard hearts often melt. Time and again I have said to tough men, full of hurt and anger, "Here, feel the weight of the cross." As they lift the cross, the power of the Holy Spirit breaks through, and I lead them in prayer as they weep. Brokenhearted people weeping with pain and grief have been healed as we talk and pray.

I always say, "Jesus did it. Jesus drew them. Jesus saved them. Jesus is present in the glory of God that the people feel."

These people come from every walk of life. They are battle-hardened soldiers who melt before the cross with tears in their eyes. They are old women and little children, eating, smiling, and feeling the love and glory of God as they gather around the cross.

It is the glory of the Lord on the battlefields, along the roadsides, and in the homes and churches of the world. The glory is present when I just walk down the road. I know that I have a glory team at all times: God who is Father, God who is Jesus, and God who is Holy Spirit! This thought alone is enough to set my feet dancing on a hot road in the desert.

The following stories give specific examples of experiencing the roads of glory as the cross is carried around the world.

Roads of Glory in England

In September 1971, I was invited to speak at the Nationwide Festival of Light in Hyde Park, London—a gathering of people seeking spiritual awakening in Britain. Many of the greatest spiritual leaders in England spoke, and I was the final speaker.

Only three weeks earlier I had arrived with the cross, not knowing anyone in Britain. But through a chain of amazing events, the British press touted me as the leader of the Jesus Movement in America, and great crowds met us wherever we went with the cross. Now I stood before about sixty thousand people.

"We want all of England, Britain, and the world to know that Jesus is alive and real!" I began. "This is not a revolution that is soon to pass, just as it is not a revolution that has just begun. Our leader is Jesus Christ. He is Lord!"

The crowd's agreement rolled like thunder through the growing darkness, and the fire of the Holy Spirit burned in my soul.

"Give your life to Christ. Love him. Proclaim him. Live with him. Let him be your Lord and Savior."

At the end of my message, I said, "I want to ask all of you to get on your knees with me right now. Repent, and ask God to fill you with his Holy Spirit. Those of you who don't know him as your Savior, ask him into your heart right now."

Then I asked everyone to lift their hands heavenward and join me in singing "The Lord's Prayer." My voice was off-key, but it didn't matter. No one could hear me as all those voices swelled in song.

The words of that familiar yet powerful prayer filled the night air: "Our Father which art in heaven, hallowed be thy name. Thy kingdom come, thy will be done, on earth as it is in heaven. Give us this day our daily bread. And forgive us our debts, as we forgive our debtors. And lead us not into temptation, but deliver us from evil. For thine is the kingdom, and the power, and the glory, forever. Amen."

I heard later that those outside the compound who were facing the raised platform saw strange shafts of light fall through the darkening park. Nothing could be seen except the light playing on those thousands of upraised hands.

After the melody of voices in prayer ended, a brooding silence fell over the crowd.

Police officers patrolling the area knelt with us, aware—as we were—of God's presence. The Holy Spirit was at work in the stillness: breaking and melting hearts, wooing and whispering to people. Lives were changed that night.

God's road of glory had moved through the bustling streets of London and penetrated the footpaths of Hyde Park. His love, mercy, and power shone down on the massive crowd, and his glory touched thousands.

Roads of Glory in East Germany

In November 1989, my son Joshua and I carried the cross into Leipzig, East Germany, just as communism was collapsing in that country and less than three weeks after the Berlin Wall was first opened. About 300,000 people had gathered to demonstrate for freedom, as they had every Monday night for several weeks. Would the Russian troops attack? What would happen?

We arrived at the square about 5:30 in the evening. People gathered around where I stood with the cross. I shouted one sentence to those around me: "I have been carrying the cross around the world and have come to join you."

Our translator then spoke in German. The people close enough to hear what she said went crazy with excitement. They began to mob me—shaking my hand, kissing me, kissing the cross. I tried to say more, but they couldn't hear because of clapping and cheering.

Joshua was trying to take pictures, but he was knocked down in the excitement. The men around us were so excited that they pulled the cross from my shoulders and lifted it up. When the massive throng saw the cross lifted up, they began to applaud. Strong men from the coal mines and steel mills began to push the cross forward to the platform. Everyone was standing, bodies pressed against each other. It was impossible to walk through such a crowd, so they passed the cross hand over hand. As the cross began to move, I lost my grip on it. For the first time ever, the cross got away from me! I stood on my tiptoes, watching it move toward the front of this crowd.

This was one of the most glorious moments in all the years of my walk around the world with the cross. The crowd exploded in cheers as the cross was lifted behind the speakers about to address the crowd. They were shouting, "The cross, the cross; lift it up; lift it up."

It took about fifteen minutes for me to catch up to the cross. The crowd then poured from the square into the streets to walk around the four-lane highway that circled the downtown area.

A leader motioned for me to come with him. I grabbed the cross and moved along the street with the sea of bodies. I had the cross on my shoulder, but a group of smiling men insisted they take the cross and move it along while it stood upright. In the face of over forty years of atheism, this was a glorious declaration by the people of East Germany. They had not rejected the cross. They had not followed atheism. They wanted the cross lifted up for the entire world to see.

For hours we walked the circle, carrying the cross with the people. They were kissing and hugging Joshua and me, shaking our hands, kissing the cross, crying, and laughing. The road of glory in Leipzig literally wound around the city.

Roads of Glory in Brazil

It was New Year's Eve 1987 in Rio de Janeiro, Brazil, and about two million people covered the sand of Copacabana Beach. In the heart of the beach area, believers had constructed two huge platforms, far enough apart that the loud speakers wouldn't conflict. It looked like a rock concert rather than some thirty thousand followers of Jesus gathering to celebrate Christ and share him with the crowds on the beach.

At about ten o'clock that night we marched from the platform to make a big circle around the beach. It was one of the wildest scenes I've ever seen. The believers were mixed in with all the other people. There were nearly naked people, people dancing, people burning incense, people chanting, people doing pagan rituals—and there was the cross.

Ken and Bill Henderson and my daughter Joy were with me. As we moved along with the cross, thousands of people walked with us. Once this crowd started moving, the momentum was like a tidal wave of people. Nothing could have stopped us. We shouted Jesus slogans in Portuguese as we headed back toward the platform. It was almost midnight when I finally arrived there with the cross.

As far as the eye could see, people were listening, then praying, then weeping and shouting. I have never preached to a crowd this large either before or since. God's glory shone on the faces before me. I am so aware that God makes all of this happen when huge crowds respond with such fervor. He pours out his glory, and people are transformed.

It was an awesome night.

Roads of Glory Every Day

There are more stories of the majestic evidence of God's glory coming down than I can write about here. The few you've just read give you a glimpse of the wonder and excitement that fill my life as I carry the cross for Jesus.

God's glory is also evident to me and those with me in ways less dramatic but no less amazing. I often face three conditions when walking with the cross: exhaustion, heat, and traffic.

Southern Nicaragua and India are just two of the places I remember being so exhausted that I was sure I couldn't continue. But the glory of the Lord would fill me and encourage me to get up and keep going or start talking.

In both Nigeria and the Solomon Islands the heat was almost unbearable. I struggled to drink enough fluids to stay hydrated. Just when I felt I was too hot to survive, I began to feel the wonderful glory again. God's glory is always with me, and when I need it most, I feel my awareness of it just bubble up to the surface of my mind.

Roads of glory all over the world are snarled with pedestrian and vehicle traffic. When the word goes ahead that I am coming with the cross, the glory of the Lord moves people and draws them to the cross. Traffic has never stopped God's mission. When I can't move forward, I start preaching where I am.

Of course, there are many places with these "opportunities," as my wife, Denise, calls them, to experience God's glory. His revealed glory is how many people come to know him personally and to know Jesus as their Savior. His glory is powerful, beyond words to describe, and transforming. When you've been in the presence of God's glory, you are changed.

And nothing stops God's glory from touching people all around the world. I have the most exciting calling, and I praise Jesus for this glory-filled life.

Roads of Glory Where You Live

For me, "the glory of God" is the manifestation of his presence. Jesus is the same yesterday, today, and forever. Jesus is in my heart and life, and his presence and his glory are unchanging. I am to be a living reflection of God's glory. The Spirit of the Lord sets me free within to reflect him. My passion is to live more and more in his likeness.

Our walk with Jesus is not to be up and down like a roller coaster, but steadily receiving his ever-increasing glory day by day, step by step.

If you are a follower of Jesus, I know that you also want to reflect his glory. As we know Jesus, follow him, love him, and see his face, we are changed. It's like looking into a mirror and not seeing your own image, but the image of Jesus. You may be saying, "Wait a minute, Arthur. I'm not seeing Jesus in my mirror."

Maybe not yet. Maybe not literally. But we all know people who look different somehow after they have been in the presence of the Lord. When you spend time with him and in his Word, living as he calls you to live, you reflect his light in your countenance. You relate to people with grace and kindness. You show a measure of his glory.

Pray as I do: *Holy Spirit, give me your freedom to live in the glory of God and in so doing glorify you and your Son, Jesus, my Lord.*

As you walk your own road of life, choose a road of glory. Follow Jesus. Stay close to him, and the glory will come.

Chapter 14

There Are <u>No</u> Walls

There is neither Jew nor Greek, slave nor free, male nor female, for you are all one in Christ Jesus.
—Galatians 3:28

IRAQ AND BABYLON

Oh Lord, I am so thrilled. I've lived one of my greatest dreams today. Carrying the cross in Babylon and through this historic street into the city! Jesus did it!

Since I was a child, I've always wanted to see this city. At college I wrote a paper about the walls of Babylon, and today I've not just seen them but carried and lifted up the cross here. Praise you, God; this is tremendous. Denise and I could feel the mighty glory of God today as we did what we were told we could not do. Denise was fearless in a dangerous place; and you, Jesus, have snatched victory from defeat.

I feel so close to Denise. Often people think of her as an accessory to me and the cross but she is a necessity! Her sharp mind, humor, and calmness in the face of opposition and danger are heart melting. I see you, Jesus, using her over and over to do things that open the way for the cross and our mission. She makes friends, and those friends help

us do the will of God. She was the key to us getting into Iraq and accomplishing this trip.

Thank you, Lord, for the awesome privilege of leading us here for your glory.

God's Voice in East Germany

After carrying the cross in West Germany, I preached at the "Berlin for Jesus" rally, held at Olympic Stadium in West Berlin in June 1981. About fifteen thousand people gathered that Saturday afternoon.

When I came to the end of my message, I said, "This stadium was built by Adolf Hitler to commemorate the 1936 Olympics. It was built to glorify man, but I am going to take this cross and carry it across this field and up the steps. We are going to raise the cross above where the torch burned."

Everyone on the platform was stunned; I had told none of them my plans. As I stepped off the stage with the cross and started walking across the playing field of the stadium, everyone stood, cheering and praising God. Then, as a friend helped me raise the cross above the base of the torch that had been lit for the 1936 Olympics, the people exploded with weeping and praise to God. The cross stood where Hitler's torch had been extinguished. What a glorious moment as we looked up at the very symbol of goodness and love conquering evil.

Two weeks after the "Berlin for Jesus" rally, my daughter Gina and I drove the highway from West Berlin to West Germany. It was lined with a fence and security installations. Drivers had to stay on this road, not leaving it to go into East Germany.

The car we were driving broke down, and in vain we tried to get it fixed or towed into West Germany. At midnight, while Gina was asleep in our camping trailer, I was lying on the floor, praying, *God, you have me here for a purpose. What is it?*

Then I felt the Lord speak. *Arthur, you've been praying about wanting to carry the cross behind the Iron Curtain and the Berlin Wall. There are no walls! The walls, the iron curtains, are in your mind. I don't have an iron curtain.*

I responded, *Lord, that word is gone from my vocabulary except to use when I'm preaching or when I write about it. I only want to believe your Word and your promises, not the teaching of others that have caused me to build walls.*

It wasn't long before I flew into Poland and carried the cross into other communist countries. My walls were gone.

No Closed Nations

Christians in the West sometimes talk about nations that are "closed" to the gospel. Though it is true that some governments and people groups are resistant to the good news of Jesus, at least as they perceive it, I think we need to be careful: Focusing on the concept of "closed nations" can send a negative message, a message that creates fear and hinders evangelism.

Believers often ask me, "When you were in such-and-such nation, didn't you feel darkness and the power of Satan?" Or, "When you met such-and-such terrorists, didn't you feel the evil?"

My reply is, "No, I felt the Father, Jesus, and the Holy Spirit!"

God is with me! The earth is the Lord's and the fullness thereof. Every step I take is upon God's earth. Every room I walk into, God is there. I will not concede any place or any person to the Devil.

We must listen not to the voices of fear, but to the voice of the Lord. We are told in God's Word, "God did not give us a spirit of timidity, but a spirit of power, of love and of self-discipline. So do not be ashamed to testify about our Lord, or ashamed of me his prisoner. But join with me in suffering for the gospel, by the power of God" (2 Timothy 1:7–8). We need to be followers of Jesus, trained to go anywhere at any time to any person with the good news of the love of Jesus and willing to suffer or even die in the service of God.

Just imagine what might happen in your life if you tore down those walls that keep you from doing all that God has for you to do. Dare to believe! God is with you—and he will be with you when your walls are removed.

Let's look at two main types of walls that keep us prisoners of our own fear.

External Walls

Walls of fear and mistrust paralyze our actions. They tell us that certain countries are off limits and that we cannot go there with the message of Jesus. They are the walls, caused by wars and conflicts, that surround territories, keeping fighting in and hope out.

Some of these walls are physical, though not necessarily made of bricks and mortar. They may be checkpoints with armed guards or barbed-wire fences. While they are physical, they are not walls that God constructed; and he can move people through them with his message, as he has done for me in many war-torn or religiously oppressed countries. I've just moved on, and what appeared to be walls were no walls at all!

Other external walls aren't seen with our eyes. We construct these walls by our prejudices. They cause hurt and tension between people of different religions, of different racial groups, and even within our own homes. These walls are judgmental, not loving.

We may go out of our way to avoid people because they don't believe as we do. It is easy for us to justify avoiding people who seem distasteful, such as alcoholics or drug addicts. But it is not the way of the cross.

These walls cripple people and cause many believers to retreat into the sanctuary of the church. Instead of being redemptive, we become critical and irrelevant. We hide from the very people who need to hear the message of Jesus. If we become insulated and isolated from the world, those people might miss the love that can change their lives.

Jesus wants us to be as he was—*in* the world without being *of* the world (see John 17:13–18).

Internal Walls

We use these walls, inside our hearts, to disqualify ourselves from serving Jesus in a powerful way. If you think you are disqualified from serving Jesus, just look in the Bible, and you will see God using people who failed greatly but found forgiveness as they repented. Think of Jesus and his love for the lost, the hurting, and the needy.

Many of these walls are deeply entrenched and difficult to think about or to acknowledge even to oneself. But they must come down.

You might say, "I've been divorced," or "I've had an abortion," or "I backslid in my faith," or "I was called to preach but I failed," or "I was called to the mission field but I didn't go," or "I've messed up my life so badly I can't serve God," or "I'm too ugly . . . too fat . . . too skinny . . . too old . . . too young . . . too timid . . . too poor . . . too rich." On and on we could go. Jesus may have called you to do something, but fear and that long list of negative self-talk have kept you from moving out.

Let's face it—most of us have walls. However, whether they are external or internal, we must not let walls divide us and separate us from others. We must not let any walls keep us from doing the will of God.

On June 12, 1987, in a famous speech delivered at Berlin's Brandenburg Gate, President Ronald Reagan demanded, "Mr. Gorbachev, tear down this wall!"

Just two years later, I was in East Germany with my son Joshua and the cross during the time when the Berlin Wall was actually coming down. I chipped pieces out of the wall myself. You can do that too. Chip away at those walls in your own life. Tear them down. Get rid of them. Be free!

I know that may be easier said than done. You may suffer from deep hurts that have caused you to build walls to protect your heart. Your parents or others close to you may have hurt you in some way and planted a seed of rejection that has grown and eaten away your value and purpose in life. You may have felt unwanted all your life. You may have been abused as a child or even as an adult. Hurt and injustice have built a wall around your heart.

Forgiveness doesn't mean that you stay in abusive relationships, but you do need to release your judgment and anger toward those who have hurt or offended you. You must forgive and let it go. God will deal justly with every person. If you hold on to the tormenting words or deeds, it will only destroy you. Jesus asks us to forgive everyone. There is no option.

Your wall could also be the result of things you did to others. Jesus wants you to be released from the guilt of how you may have hurt another person. Ask him to forgive you—and to show you if you need to seek the forgiveness of someone you have violated.

It's Time to Let Go

I ask you to think right now about your walls.

I suggest you go and get a tissue. Place the tissue for a moment on your chest, representing your heart and your emotions; then place it on your head, representing your mind and your memories. Let the tears flow. Wipe your eyes with the tissue. Then wad it up in your hand. Let the pain go, and invite Jesus in to cleanse and heal. Tell Jesus that you forgive anyone who ever hurt you. Ask him to forgive you for all the people you have hurt. Ask Jesus to tear down your walls and give you fresh life, love, peace, and joy.

Hold that tissue until you feel release. Then praise God while you throw the tissue into the toilet and flush it away, never to be retrieved.

Keep your eyes on Jesus, and live in the freedom of "no walls."

We See No Walls and We Move On

The following accounts are of a few of the places where Denise and I have carried the cross even though they were considered "closed." You will see how God led us right through man-made walls and enabled us to tell people about Jesus.

Iraq

Between 1990 and 1997 Denise and I tried several times to get visas to Iraq; but with my U.S. passport and Denise's British passport we were always refused. In April 1998, we flew into Amman, Jordan, determined to go to Iraq. Throughout these years, the United Nations had imposed strict economic sanctions on the country.

Again the Iraqi embassy in Amman denied us visas.

We refused to give up. We prayed, and the Lord blessed us with a driver to take us through the desert for about two hundred miles to the Jordanian-Iraqi border in the heart of the Muslim Middle East.

Near the border we had our driver, Amer, stop so I could bolt together the cross and begin walking. I told Amer we would like him to go with us as our interpreter. He was a Muslim, and we had been sharing Jesus with him. Agreeing to help us, Amer went ahead of us to speak to the Jordanian border guards. When Denise and I arrived with the cross, we were welcomed as pilgrims of God. We met the commander of the border station, who said, "Since you are on a haj to pray for God's peace and blessing, you may go."

We walked through the border and about a mile and a half farther to the first Iraqi checkpoint. Amer explained our mission and said I wanted to pray just inside the checkpoint. The soldiers consented. Denise and I stepped off the highway, and I leaned the cross against a fence just past a huge arch with a mammoth-sized painting of Saddam Hussein. Lying in the sand, I prayed for about ten minutes.

While I prayed, Denise showed the guards the photo album of our travels around the world with the cross, including photos with Muslim leaders like Yasser Arafat. When I got up, I saw that a crowd of men had gathered around me. Muslims bow to pray toward Mecca in Saudi Arabia, but they had never seen a cross-carrying man lying flat on the ground, praying toward Iraq.

The guards gave us a pack of cigarettes and two cold Pepsis, and they said to wait a few minutes. They had taken the photo album to the border post ahead. After a while they said, "The head of security and the border post commander want to welcome you at the VIP reception hall. They will send a car."

We explained that we were on a mission to walk with the cross and so would prefer to walk there. A soldier accompanied us to the building about half a mile ahead.

There Denise and I were greeted warmly. Tea was brought to us as we sat on a couch. The chief of security welcomed us and gave us about a dozen poster-sized photos of Saddam Hussein.

"You are welcome in Iraq. We are happy you have come to pray. We need more people like you."

We had a long talk as I showed him our photo album and explained the message of the cross. He said he was sorry we did not have a visa.

I gripped the official's hand, looked him in the eyes, and said, "You can get us in! God has you here, and your mission is to get us into Baghdad and Babylon."

He then explained how we could get a visa, hoping we would return to Iraq soon. I prayed with him and all in the room. We said goodbye and carried the cross back to the border and into Jordan.

Two months later Denise and I returned to Jordan on the way back to Iraq. We were invited as special guests to attend an event called "The Third Christian Conference in Iraq," which had as its theme "The church in the service of peace and humanity." Our invitation was from former Air Vice-Marshal Georges Sada, who was chairman of the preparatory committee. The head of security at the border post had arranged for us to get a visa by having Sada extend this invitation to us.

We joined a group of pastors and church leaders in Amman and were driven by bus several hundred miles to Baghdad. Hundreds of believers gathered in the assembly hall of the Babylon Hotel for morning and evening sessions. Every major Christian group—Catholics, Orthodox, Protestants—was at the conference.

People from the area that is now Iraq were present at Pentecost, just after the ascension of Jesus, and were saved, filled with the Holy Spirit, and returned to this land. Churches have been in Iraq for almost two thousand years. We hear a lot about the Shiite and Sunni Muslims in Iraq, but about 3 percent of the population is Christian. How thrilling to meet and embrace our fellow followers of Jesus.

The government welcomed us and the cross. The police and army and the people in customs and immigration all treated us warmly.

Babylon

One of my greatest dreams in life was to lift the cross atop the ruins of Babylon and carry it in that ancient city. Babylon is referred to in the Book of Revelation as the seat of Satan and is important in "end-time" events. I *know* Jesus wanted the cross carried there.

People at the conference told us that Babylon, about fifty miles south of Baghdad, was closed to tourists. We arranged for a car to drive us there anyway. We tied the cross, in its bag, on top of the car. When we arrived at Babylon, we took off the bag and bolted the cross together. The driver was shocked but excited when we showed him photos of the cross with Yasser Arafat and other world leaders. He showed the photos to the officials, who then rushed to help us. I started carrying the cross, but soon our driver and the other men were competing to carry it.

We carried the cross through the remains of the Ishtar Gate and along the Street of Procession. The actual street was fenced off, but the men helped me over the fence so I could carry the cross where Daniel and Nebuchadnezzar walked.

Denise and I carried the cross into the ruins of Nebuchadnezzar's palace. Here the "handwriting on the wall," which Daniel was called to interpret, appeared to King Belshazzar. We raised the cross up against the ruins of that wall.

For hours we carried the cross through the remains of ancient Babylon, raising the cross above the large stone sculpture of the Lion of Babylon, created some 2,600 years ago.

We then went along the Euphrates River to an unexcavated area where we could see the foundation ruins of what may have been the Tower of Babel, mentioned in Genesis 11. We walked to the mound of earth overlooking the site. Denise and I held the cross up and prayed. Babel represented the supreme achievement of humanity against God; now the cross had been raised above what may be its ruins.

Ur of the Chaldeans

While in Iraq, we visited Ur, referred to in the Bible as "Ur of the Chaldeans." This is the city where Abraham was born and where God spoke to him, saying, "Leave your country, your people and your father's household and go to the land I will show you. I will make you into a great nation and I will bless you; I will make your name great, and you will be a blessing" (Genesis 12:1–2). From this place and from

Abraham came three of the world's great religions: Judaism, Islam, and Christianity.

We made the 250-mile trip from Baghdad to Ur, near the Kuwaiti border, by bus. The temperature rose above 120 degrees.

We were so blessed to have the privilege of carrying the cross where God called Abraham and from where the nations of the world have been blessed. We also went to a ziggurat, a temple tower of the ancient Assyrians and Babylonians having the form of a terraced pyramid. Built about four thousand years ago, the ziggurat is still well preserved in large part. Denise felt led to carry the cross there, so I took only a few symbolic steps.

It was an awesome trip to Iraq—and truly there were no walls!

China

The Great Wall of China stretches for thousands of miles across this vast country, and for more than two thousand years, it has been one of the great wonders of the world. On January 5, 1987, my feet stood on the Great Wall with the cross lifted up in this communist nation. What a historic moment in the journey of the cross!

The news reporters were on the wall to welcome the "world's greatest walker," not the simple "cross-walker." No one knew I was carrying a cross.

The man organizing the walk was getting cold feet and seemed to be backing out. Jack Hunter, a dear friend traveling with me, and I prayed and got in touch with a man we met the night before who offered to help in the event of any trouble. He turned out to be a top official, and he took care of all the challenges we faced. Jesus had us meet the right person to overcome the "wall" of walking with the cross on China's Great Wall.

North Korea

After almost ten years of seeking a visa for the hard-line communist country of North Korea, we finally got permission to go. This trip would complete the mission of carrying the cross in every sovereign nation on earth. Our excitement was almost uncontainable.

Denise and I flew into Beijing, China, and went to the North Korean embassy there. The ambassador gave us our visas in red-velvet folders. When we arrived at the North Korean border, three officials and a driver welcomed us. They treated us with great kindness and respect.

The customs officers wanted to know what the wood was for. "I carry the wood and do walks with it," I said. They seemed to think I was just a strange American sportsman and let us through.

Our visit was in the Rajin-Sonbong Economic Special Zone, where North Korea joins both China and Russia.

Sunday morning, August 30, 1998, Denise and I carried the cross from our hotel to Pipha Island and returned on the main road. The cross had now been carried in every nation on earth. I had fulfilled Jesus' call on my life to carry the cross in every country before the year 2000. Jesus did it! Denise and I were so excited. I was almost overcome by emotion. Lying on the ground, I prayed for the Lord to bless North Korea and its beautiful people.

There were "no walls" separating us from the people Jesus wanted us to reach. The world had been open to the cross, and we lived to tell the story.

The Freedom of "No Walls!"

My son Joshua is an evangelist based in Norway. As he and I were planning some meetings together, he sent to me a suggested news release that truly expresses "no walls." He wrote, "I have spent a lifetime watching my father *do* what others say is impossible and *go* where people have said he can't go!"

With no walls, a person is ready and free to be used by Jesus for the glory of God in the power of the Holy Spirit.

What about you? What's holding you back from tearing those walls down and keeping them down?

Remember that tissue you flushed away? You couldn't pick it up again if you tried. Keep those walls down, and move ahead to the glorious freedom of doing the will of God. What a journey is in store for you!

Chapter 15

Giving God Your Best

Whatever you do, work at it with all your heart,
as working for the Lord, not for men.
—*Colossians 3:23*

BASEL 1987

Oh Lord Jesus, you have just asked me to do one of the hardest things I've ever had to do. You want me to give up my dreams, but, Lord, you

gave them to me! These grand ideas of the way you would use me have battled to control me. As I pray I realize that these dreams have become idols almost. They have been motivating me and binding me. Oh Lord, I want only you to control me! I understand that you need to rip this away from my heart and mind. Go ahead and do it, Lord. I want your will, your way, your love, your peace, your message, your salvation, and your life. It's all about you, Jesus. It's not my idea of what your will looks like for me. Oh Jesus, I want your will even if I too must sweat in agony as you did in the garden.

I give my dreams up, Lord! Wow, I feel astoundingly free. I feel calm. I have the simple knowledge that whatever you desire for me is enough. I accept whatever you send. Your will does not have to conform to any of my preconceived

conditions. I am free in the Spirit. Glory!

I t was another required chapel service at Mississippi College in 1959, and I felt certain the gray-haired man sitting on the stage would be a boring speaker with nothing meaningful to say to the other students and me.

I sat in the back of the auditorium so I could study one of my textbooks. I paid little attention as the speaker was introduced and as he struggled to his feet and walked slowly to the podium, which he gripped with all his might to support his tottering frame. But this man grabbed my attention as he began talking about his struggles as a missionary in China during the great persecution of believers about a decade earlier. He had been imprisoned and saw many pastors and friends killed for following Jesus.

As he spoke of these trials and sufferings, I noticed what seemed to be a heavenly glow on his face. And even though he spoke of horrible tragedies, he had a loving smile on his face as he spoke about Jesus being with him in all the events of his life. But it was his closing challenge to us students that had the greatest impact on me and still sticks with me nearly half a century later.

"Jesus is worthy of your best, or nothing!" he said. "Jesus is worth going with all the way, or he is not worth following at all!"

After hearing this gentle servant of God, I made a solemn vow to the Lord that, no matter what Jesus called me to do, I would go with him all the way, wherever he led me, and give him my best for the rest of my life.

Since then my commitment to give God my best has influenced every area of my life—from small things to big things. I would like to share what this has meant to me. I'm not doing so to draw attention to myself or to make myself look like a spiritual superstar. Rather, I want to challenge *you* to give your best to God in whatever you do. Or, as Paul told the Christians in Colosse, "Whatever you do, work at it with all your heart, as working for the Lord, not for men" (Colossians 3:23).

Giving My Best to the Many and the Few

I am frequently asked to speak in churches or at other events. I accept as many of these invitations as I can, regardless of how many people will be there. I give my best no matter where I am or how big the crowd is—whether I'm speaking to thousands of people at a prestigious church or to a humble peasant selling vegetables at a roadside market in the most remote area on earth.

Just before I speak, I always look up and remember the face of Jesus. No matter who is present, I know Jesus is there—so I must give my best.

Giving My Best to the Rich and the Poor

I was in Basel, Switzerland, in 1987 when Jesus clearly spoke these words to my heart: *Lie down on the sidewalk and give up your dreams.*

I was afraid the police might arrest me for obeying this command, but I decided I would rather be arrested than disobey. There on the sidewalk, I wrestled with Jesus. *But you gave me these dreams. These dreams are so important to me.*

Then Jesus said, *I gave you these dreams; I can also take them away.*

I couldn't remember ever feeling so spiritually empty and void.

No dreams? I asked both Jesus and myself. *What will I do?*

Jesus replied, *Let your dream be no bigger than the next person you meet. Give them everything!*

I understood Jesus to say that I was not to let my dreams stand in the way of giving my best to him by giving my best to every person I would meet. I am not to judge who is worthy of my time or attention. I am to lavish these on everyone.

I love the passage about the sheep and the goats in Matthew 25. Jesus is telling his disciples about caring for the poor, the prisoner, the downcast, and the downtrodden. "I tell you the truth," he says, "whatever you did for one of the least of these brothers of mine, you did for me."

I saw this passage come to life while walking with my son Joshua through South Africa. As we walked along a road, a poor man took off his hat and bowed to us. Before I knew how to respond, Joshua took off his hat and bowed to the man. Tears come to my eyes even now as I think about Joshua's beautiful response to the man's beautiful gesture.

How we treat the poorest and the neediest among us is a good gauge of how we treat Jesus. I am constantly confronted with Jesus as I meet the homeless, the hungry, the thirsty, the prisoner, and others throughout the world.

How we treat the poor is also a barometer of our love for God. Many people express their love to God through worship during a church service. But we also show our love for God by treating others the same way we would treat Jesus if we could see him in our midst. It's no good if we praise God in church and then gripe at the waitress who serves us in a restaurant after church. It's no good if we act righteous on Sunday but on Monday turn away from the homeless man or woman we see sitting on a bench.

The greatest needs any of us has are the needs for hope and love and to know that God cares for us. I can share these gifts with each person who crosses my path, as I try to give God my best.

Giving God My Best through My Work

My job is an unusual one: carrying a cross around the world. But as I carry out this calling, I try to give God my best by doing my best.

When I take the cross with me to speak at a church, it is tempting to merely tighten the bolts with my fingers instead of using tools to tighten them all the way. But that wouldn't be giving my best. Instead, I grab two wrenches and tighten each bolt as firmly as I would if I were preparing to carry the cross a thousand miles. These aren't just pieces of wood held together by metal. Jesus died on a cross for the salvation of humanity; putting together this cross is an act of devotion that is worthy of my best.

As I walk the roads of the world, I seek to carry the cross with honor. I hold my shoulders back and my head up. This is good for my health and posture, of course. But more importantly, this is important as I strive to give my best to Jesus and to all the people who look at me as I pass by.

I look people in the eye as I walk. I smile at them. I speak to them with love and kindness. I show respect for each person I meet, because every one of them has been created in the image of God (Genesis 1:26). I use the word *sir* when I'm speaking to a terrorist and the word *ma'am* when I'm talking to a prostitute, because these individuals are precious in Jesus' sight. My prayer is that what they see through my attitude may leave a lasting and positive impression of the love, mercy, and compassion of Jesus.

Giving God My Best by Keeping Going

Mount Fuji, towering 12,388 feet above the sea in a massive cone, is a majestic and beautiful symbol of Japan. During our visit to Japan in 1991, it took three days of climbing thirty-two miles up a winding road just to reach the fifth stage at a height of about 7,500 feet.

Denise joined me on foot for the major climb to the top. She carried our backpack as I carried the cross higher and higher up this dormant volcano, which is covered with volcanic boulders and fine ash. The air got thinner as we climbed, but we kept going because Jesus had called us to carry the cross up Mount Fuji, and we wanted to give God our best.

As we made our way up the mountainside, we were joined by two platoons of U.S. Marines from Japanese bases who were making the climb at the same time. These kind young men often helped me get up and over a tough place with the cross. We continued to climb, past boulders and snow, as the air grew colder and dense clouds swept past us.

On the final ascent, in the toughest area, a group of six marines was resting where we stopped. They volunteered to help me get the cross to the top. "We'll raise it up at the top like the marines did with the flag on Iwo Jima!" they said.

They carried the cross with three or four at a time holding it. It exhausted us all, but we finally made it. The cross of Jesus was uplifted atop Mount Fuji!

Perhaps you have heard the marine slogan: "The few, the proud, the Marines." Marines pride themselves on their dedication and commitment. It was thrilling to walk alongside them, and as we did so, we thought even more about our own commitment to give God our best as we walked with the cross.

Giving God My Best by Seeking to Be the Least

When I attended the presidential prayer breakfast in Washington, D.C., in 1988, I met Piet G. J. Koornhof, South Africa's ambassador to the United States. I had just carried the cross in South Africa, so he invited me into his elegant office.

Ambassador Koornhof showed me many beautiful items and gifts he had received during his years of public service, but my eye was drawn to a humble-looking item. "Sir, what is that?" I asked.

He made no immediate response, but I could see tears filling his eyes. Then he spoke.

"I want to tell you a story," he said. "One day I was officiating at the opening of a South African market for native crafts. There were many beautiful items made of gold and ivory on display. After my speech, the craftspeople told me I could have as a gift anything I wanted. I chose that item you see now. It is a straw donkey. I have had it in my offices ever since.

"It may seem out of place with the fine things in this office, but it is a reminder to me that we serve a Lord and Savior who rode into Jerusalem on a donkey instead of a beautiful white horse or an expensive chariot. I resolved to give my life being a donkey for Jesus, so that whatever I do people will focus on Jesus and not me."

A lot of people today talk about being "upwardly mobile." But that day, as I spoke to the ambassador, we both could see that God wants his servants to be "downwardly mobile."

Giving God my best doesn't mean I always *get* the best. But no matter what I get, which is out of my control, I will always *give* my best—which is something I can control.

We Are Capable

Maybe you are saying, "I would never be able to carry a cross." But maybe you could.

To my knowledge, at the time I carried a cross from coast to coast in 1969, no one had ever done such a thing. In the years since, however, many people have carried a cross extensively or done cross-walks near their church or around their city. My son Joshua is an evangelist and does cross-walks in connection with evangelism training in churches around the world. My daughter Gina also uses a cross in outreach evangelism in Denver and other places.

A more important question to consider than the question of carrying a physical cross is this: Whatever God has called you to do, are you doing it with all your heart and all your soul and all your mind? Are you giving God your best?

Some people say they aren't capable of doing anything great or worthwhile; but that is the gravest error anyone could make.

Recently I brought the closing message on a TBN television broadcast that featured a group of people whom many would call "handicapped." But host Paul Crouch Jr. called them "handi-capable." These people had severe disabilities, such as being born without legs or arms. Others were blind or paralyzed. All of them, however, were in full-time ministry—serving Jesus with all their hearts. These people were radiant and joyful in the face of huge challenges. They were giving Jesus their best.

Whatever our challenge may be, it doesn't change our commission. We are to give God our best.

Jesus Is Worth Our Best

I love to give my best because Jesus is worthy of my best, as we see in this beautiful passage from the Book of Revelation:

> In a loud voice they sang:
> "Worthy is the Lamb, who was slain,
> to receive power and wealth and wisdom and strength
> and honor and glory and praise!"

Then I heard every creature in heaven and on earth and under the earth and on the sea, and all that is in them, singing:
"To him who sits on the throne and to the Lamb
be praise and honor and glory and power,
for ever and ever!" (Revelation 5:12–13)

Friends, when we get to heaven, we will join to sing praises to Jesus, because he is truly worthy. Isn't he worth our best while we walk on the earth he created and serve the people created in his image?

If you agree that he is worthy, then join me in giving him your best. No matter what you do, do it for him with everything you have!

Chapter 16

Into the Arms of Jesus

Come to me, all you who are weary and burdened,
and I will give you rest.
—Matthew 11:28

MAN IN HOLLAND

The events of today keep filling my mind, and I feel such complex emotions. It's been a horrendous struggle of life and blood. I held a man in the battle to either live or die. His blood has stained my clothes and hands, but I cannot wash the pain away. I keep looking at my hands and wondering how to be my brother's keeper.

I want to be the emergency crew for the bruised and broken along the roads of life. The burden for the world that is within me is far harder to carry than the wooden cross. I feel the pain; I touch the people and live with them in this world. Oh Jesus, this is the night for weeping and caring for the lost and hurting. May I be an instrument of your peace, salvation, and life. So often we are blind to others' greatest needs. I

remember, Jesus, when you were in the garden the night before your crucifixion, you asked three of your disciples to go with you to watch and pray, yet they kept falling asleep. Oh Lord God, may I not sleep when someone needs me; keep me awake to your will and be able to see the world through your eyes.

Baptize me in your passion, Jesus, and baptize me with the fire of your love that truly makes me my brother's keeper in every way. I lift your cross up, Jesus, knowing you will draw all to yourself. I pray for a mighty move of your Spirit to empower your children to share the message of Jesus with others. Send forth your laborers into the harvest! I close my eyes now, and I can see the harvest of the world coming in Glory!

Fall into Safety

Much of my life has been lived walking alongside the roads of the world. Danger from traffic is ever present as cars and trucks rush by just inches away from my body. The roadsides are littered with bottles, rocks, sticks, and other rubble, making it difficult to walk.

When carrying the cross along the road, I always plan, if I should stumble, to fall away from the road and not into the traffic. It's become an automatic response for me: the second I realize I'm about to stumble or fall, I lean away from the road. There might not be traffic at that moment, but just imagine what could happen to me if there were!

The same is true for all of us on the road of life. Leaning one way can lead to danger, and leaning the other way can lead to safety. When I stumble on life's roadways, I want to fall into the arms of Jesus—not away from him.

The roads we walk are filled with the dangers of temptation and deceit. These stumbling stones and vines can trip us up on our walk with the Lord. Our desire should be never to stumble or fall but to live in the perfect way of Jesus. Yet, should you stumble, always fall away from the dangers of drugs, drink, depression, anger, past addictions, and anything else that might take you away from Jesus. Fall into his arms, where there is hope, strength, security, love, mercy, and life. Fall into grace. Fall into love. Jesus loves you. God isn't mad at you; he cares for you.

The very second you sense the temptation to fall away from him, lean the other way. Remember what he says in his Word. Pray. Stop and think about what you're about to do. Before you take one step in the wrong direction, turn around. Picture Jesus with outstretched arms, welcoming you into his embrace of safety.

Jesus Stands Ready to Catch You

Even children can fall into the arms of Jesus. That's where it started for me.

The year was 1947, and I was seven years old. A church in the rural community of Goodwill, Louisiana, had erected a temporary shelter called a brush arbor. Sawdust had been scattered on the ground, and wooden pews had been brought in.

The evangelist preached about Jesus, and for the first time in my young life, I felt spiritually lost and in need of forgiveness. I wanted to invite Jesus into my life. I wanted to fall into his arms. I started to go to the front when the minister called for people to come and pray. But my mother, thinking I didn't understand what was being asked of me, wouldn't let me do so.

On the way home after the meeting, I asked my mother why she wouldn't let me give my heart to Jesus. My dad stopped the truck and turned around. It was dark when we arrived back at the meeting place. The lights were off, but I saw the evangelist and the pastor getting into a car. I ran to the evangelist and told him I knew I was a sinner, I wanted Jesus to save me, and I wanted to live for Jesus all my life.

That man of God knelt in the dirt and explained to me how I could know Jesus, and then he said he would lead me in a prayer. I repeated a simple prayer asking Jesus to forgive my sins and come into my life. I knew in that moment that Jesus washed my sins away as I fell into his arms. My soul was at peace and has been ever since.

Asking Jesus into your heart is the first step in walking with him the rest of your life. In the next chapter I'll give those of you who have never invited Jesus into your life an opportunity to do just that. For now, I want you to imagine falling into his arms. This is a metaphor for trusting him, and trust is essential when you invite him into your heart and decide to live as his follower. Trust overcomes fear. Trust brings joy. Trust in Jesus will change your life.

The following stories are about people from various parts of the world who chose to fall into the arms of Jesus and receive those blessings.

Poland

In 1983 I walked through Poland as thousands of people followed the cross. One day when I stopped for a break and was sitting under a tree, a young woman came running to me, talking rapidly. I asked my interpreter what she was saying. "She heard that you know how to find Jesus," he replied.

I noticed that both of the young women's legs were bleeding. "What's wrong with her legs?" I asked the interpreter.

"Do you see that hill over there and the people climbing it on their knees? She has been climbing that hill on her knees to show her love for Christ. Someone just told her that the man with the cross knows how to talk with Jesus, so she has come to see if you can tell her how to find him."

I discovered that her name was Anna and that she was twenty-four years old. She had short blond hair and beautiful clear eyes. Tears streamed down her face as she sat there with bloody legs.

I said to Anna, through the interpreter, "Jesus loved you before you ever started up that hill, and he loves you now that you have come down. All your blood was unnecessary. He has already shed his blood for you. Now I know that Jesus appreciates your desire to show him your love, but you don't have to do that to prove you love him. He can live in your heart."

I explained to Anna how Christ died for, and was offering to her, the gift of salvation. She could pray to invite Jesus into her heart, and he would become her Savior. I led Anna in a short prayer. Then she leaped into my lap and hugged me, crying and smiling. Then she jumped up and started to run away.

"Wait, wait. Come back!" I called.

She turned and said, "I have found Jesus. I found him; now I know him. That is all I need. Now I can go. I've found him! I've found him!" And she ran away.

Anna understood that she no longer had to climb that hill on her knees for Jesus to love and accept her. She trusted him. She fell into his arms.

You don't have to prove your sorrow for sin by self-inflicted punishment. Jesus has already borne your sins and carried your sorrows. Trust him and invite him in.

Switzerland

One day in 1984, while I was carrying the cross in Switzerland, I struck up a conversation with a businessman. When I said to him, "Jesus loves you," the man replied, "I hope so."

"I have good news for you," I said, and then I shared the gospel with him. I'll never forget his response when I said to him, "Jesus wants to come into your heart."

"Oh no. If he looked into my heart, what he'd see would be so bad he would not dare to enter—nor would he want to enter."

Tears filled my eyes as I invited him to the house where I was spending the night.

That evening he received a clean heart as Christ came to live within him. He saw that Jesus invites everyone to trust him and follow him. He leaned away from his belief that Jesus would reject him and into the arms outstretched to hold him.

South Africa

During my cross-walk in South Africa, we had a great "Rally for Jesus" in Cape Town. People of all races gathered to worship the Lord. My cross was leaning against the platform. While we sang, I noticed a man sitting near the front. I could tell he was blind, since it was apparent he had no eyeballs.

I left the platform, went to the man, and asked him if he spoke English. When he replied that he did, I told him who I was and invited him to come feel the cross, since he couldn't see it. He said he would like that.

I led the man to the cross, and then I watched something amazing happen. He touched the cross in a tender and loving way like I had never seen it touched before. He seemed to be crying, but without tears. He felt the cross all the way to the bottom. It was so moving that the entire audience wept.

This blind man brought passion and freshness to the meaning of the cross. The man without eyes saw things most people are blind to. It was obvious whom he trusted. This man had already chosen to follow Jesus, and he lived in the safety of his embrace.

New Zealand

While we were near Wellington, New Zealand, on a cold day in 1995, I carried the cross along a highway beside the beach. I noticed a young lady in jogging clothes running in the sand on the beach. Soon after, I started carrying the cross up a steep, narrow road into the mountains.

Suddenly I heard someone calling me. I looked up to see the young woman in the jogging suit in front of me. She had emerged from a trail up ahead and was running toward me on the road.

"Why are you carrying that cross?" she asked. She was short of breath and seemed anxious to hear my answer.

I explained my mission of walking with the cross around the world.

The woman then told me she had been living near the beach for about two years. She shared that life had become unbearable. She had planned to run into the sea that day and drown. She was going for her final run.

She said she stopped and cried to God: *I need life.* Just then she looked up and saw the cross!

"I have come to the cross!" she declared. Then the young woman burst into tears.

I talked to her about the love and mercy and salvation of Jesus. We prayed together, and she repented and gave her heart and life to Jesus. It was glorious.

I will never forget what she then said: "Now I have life!"

Like so many other desperate people, this precious young woman turned away from ending her life and fell into the arms of Jesus.

Holland

I had been carrying the cross through Holland in 1983. One morning I was ministering in the streets of Amsterdam with Youth With A Mission. Near a tram stop a young woman on our team came running up and pleaded, "Arthur, Arthur, you are needed over here. Come quickly!"

She led me and others on our team to a crowd of people watching a man trying to kill himself. He had run his arm through a plate-glass window, and blood was pouring out of his arm. He was beating his head against a big steel container.

I tried to grab him and cut off the flow of blood from his arm. He turned toward me with his other arm coiled back, ready to hit me. He was about thirty years old and was strong and muscular.

We said, "You don't have to kill yourself. Jesus died for you; he loves you."

He responded by cursing. He kept turning to beat his head. We grabbed him again, and he again drew back his arm, ready to hit us. His blood was gushing.

Finally I said to him, "Listen, we are not going to let you die here. These other people can watch you die, but we love you. We are going to grab your arm and cut off the flow of blood. If you want to beat us to death, we will die with you; but we are not going to let you die alone. Jesus has already shed his blood for you, and you don't have to shed your blood to kill yourself. He has already died to save you."

He looked at me, drew back his fist, and then fell into my arms—crying like a baby. After a brief explanation, I led him in a prayer to invite Christ into his heart. He was in the arms of Jesus now.

This man finally gave up his attempts to end a life that had trusted in nothing secure and had lost all hope. He was safe. He had fallen in the right direction, and new hope was in his future.

We Who Know Jesus Are Called to Show Others the Way

An ambulance arrived, and some of the ministry team went with the man, still bleeding profusely, to the hospital. I had blood all over me, so I went to my room to take a bath.

When I got to my room, I washed my hands in the sink. The blood on my hands washed away by the water from the faucet. I remembered how Pilate tried to wash his hands of the blood of Jesus. It seemed like the Lord was saying to me, *Arthur, you can't wash your hands of the blood of a lost, sick, dying world.*

Tears filled my eyes as I thought, *We are responsible for them. We can't isolate ourselves into spiritual clubs full of joy and praise but with no involvement in a hurting and painful world. We must be in the world but not of the world. Jesus didn't remain in heaven—because the love of God demanded action. Jesus came in the flesh; he got involved. So must we.*

How many of us try to wash our hands of the world—watching, like the crowd on that street in Amsterdam, while others die? O God, have mercy on us! Let us be there to embrace a hurting world with the love of Jesus.

No one is too sinful or too far gone. God will hear the prayer of anyone who wants to know him, whether that person is a Muslim, a Jew, a Hindu, a Buddhist, an atheist, or a member of a Christian church who doesn't have a relationship with Jesus. The only prayer God rejects is one from the self-righteous, as Jesus showed us in the parable of the Pharisee and the tax collector.

> Two men went up to the temple to pray, one a Pharisee and the other a tax collector. The Pharisee stood up and prayed about himself: "God, I thank you that I am not like other men—robbers, evildoers, adulterers—or even like this tax collector. I fast twice a week and give a tenth of all I get."
>
> But the tax collector stood at a distance. He would not even look up to heaven, but beat his breast and said, "God, have mercy on me, a sinner."
>
> I tell you that this man, rather than the other, went home justified before God. For everyone who exalts himself will be humbled, and he who humbles himself will be exalted. (Luke 18:10–14)

We are called to tell everyone about Jesus, even the self-righteous. If they still choose to turn away from the love and safety of the arms of Jesus, that is their choice. But at least they will have heard the truth of the gospel.

It is not for us to judge who will follow and who will not. It is for us to point the way of the cross along the road of life. It is for us to show others how to lean into the arms of Jesus, away from the dangerous traffic that can harm them.

The next chapter is an invitation to follow Jesus. If you have never invited Jesus into your life, the next two pages may be the most important ones you will ever read. Please read on.

Chapter 17

Come Just as You Are

For God so loved the world that he gave his one and only Son, that whoever believes in him shall not perish but have eternal life.
—John 3:16

God's Invitation

J ohn 3:16, printed above, is probably the most well-known verse in Scripture. Sometimes you'll even see an enthusiastic follower of Jesus on a televised football game waving a sign with "John 3:16" written on it.

John 3:16 is very familiar.

But is it personal for *you*?

A Personal Invitation to You

On this historic journey around the world I have issued invitations to people to follow Jesus, and I have prayed the blessings of God upon individuals and families and nations. I would like to offer this invitation to you. Today, right now, I want to lead you in a prayer inviting Jesus to come into your life.

This is a simple prayer, but it will be the beginning of a new life. You will be born again into the kingdom and family of God. Jesus will give you eternal life. His presence will be with you always.

Just as if you were standing by the cross on a roadside, please pray these words to God:

> Dear God, as best I know how, I give you my life. Lord Jesus Christ, Son of God, have mercy on me, a sinner. I open my heart and invite you, Jesus, to come and live in me. I repent of my sins and ask you to wash them away through your holy blood shed on the cross. Write my name in your book in heaven. Fill me with the Holy Spirit. I want to follow you all the days of my life. Fill me with your love and presence as I forgive everyone I need to forgive. I am not ashamed of you, Lord Jesus, and I now confess you as my Savior.
>
> In Jesus' name I pray.

I encourage you, now as a follower of Jesus, to pray the following prayer:

Dear God, I love you. Not my will—but your will—be done. Take out of me anything that does not look like Jesus. Put in me everything that does look like Jesus. Fill me with the fruit of the Holy Spirit: love, joy, peace, patience, kindness, goodness, faithfulness, gentleness, and self-control. Free me from fear; tear down any walls in my heart and mind; fill me with love for others. I welcome the power of the Holy Spirit to use and guide me in being powerful, sensitive, and effective in sharing Jesus with others, wherever you lead me.

May I hear your voice clearly and do your will perfectly. I welcome your will for my life; give me the power to do it. Help me to love others as you have loved me. Here am I, Lord. Send me.

In Jesus' name, amen.

One of my favorite things to do as I meet people is to bless them. I have prayed for countless numbers of people around the world as I bless them in Jesus' name. Time and distance are no problem with God, so as I have done with people in every nation, I pray this prayer of blessing over you and your family:

The Lord bless you and keep you.

The Lord make his face to shine upon you and give you his peace, blessings, and love.

May he bless your going out and your coming in from this day forth and forevermore.

May he give you his health and prosper you in all things.

May the love of God and the grace of the Lord Jesus Christ and the communion of the Holy Spirit be with now and forevermore. Amen.

For More Information

I would like to invite you to visit our website: www.Blessitt.com.

There, in the "Inspiration and Witness" section, you can find help in following Jesus and in sharing Jesus with others. You can also read my weekly columns and my online blog.

Stories and photos of walking with the cross in every nation are posted. We have an online store that includes DVDs of us carrying the cross around the world, with original footage, as well as discipleship and evangelism training materials.

The "Travel Tips" section includes practical suggestions for walking, buying shoes and boots, international travel, and links to helpful travel websites.

I also invite you to write, call, or e-mail me. I would love to hear how God has encouraged or challenged you through this book.

God bless you!

A pilgrim follower of Jesus,

Arthur Blessitt
Luke 18:1

P.O. Box 201840
Denver, Colorado 80220
(303) 283-7415
arthur@blessitt.com

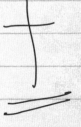